Heal Your
Sacred Sexual Self

Emotional & Spiritual Healing
for Sexual Dis-ease

Adam and Dawnee Loya

BALBOA.
PRESS

A DIVISION OF HAY HOUSE

Balboa Press books may be ordered through booksellers or by contacting:

Balboa Press
A Division of Hay House
1663 Liberty Drive
Bloomington, IN 47403
www.balboapress.com
1 (877) 407-4847

Because of the dynamic nature of the Internet, any web addresses or links contained in this book may have changed since publication and may no longer be valid. The views expressed in this work are solely those of the author and do not necessarily reflect the views of the publisher, and the publisher hereby disclaims any responsibility for them.

The author of this book does not dispense medical advice or prescribe the use of any technique as a form of treatment for physical, emotional, or medical problems without the advice of a physician, either directly or indirectly. The intent of the author is only to offer information of a general nature to help you in your quest for emotional and spiritual well-being. In the event you use any of the information in this book for yourself, which is your constitutional right, the author and the publisher assume no responsibility for your actions.

Any people depicted in stock imagery provided by Thinkstock are models, and such images are being used for illustrative purposes only. Certain stock imagery © Thinkstock.

Printed in the United States of America.

ISBN: 978-1-4525-8491-1 (sc)
ISBN: 978-1-4525-8492-8 (e)

Library of Congress Control Number: 2013918554

Balboa Press rev. date: 11/11/2013

"Sex is a meditation.
Learn the art of it.
Savour it.
Prepare for it.
Become sensitive, silent, open.
When you are going into lovemaking,
you are entering the Temple.
Enter only when you are prayerful—
then you know
the secret of sex . . .
laughter belongs to life.
Let sex be playful, fun."
Osho

Dedication

We pledged February 14, 2013 to rise up
with 1 Billion Rising
offering Divine Love light
to all sexual dis-ease.

May all benefit
without one exception.

We offer our gratitude

to all who guide us, especially: Margot Anand, Mantak Chia, Eve
     Eisler, Shakti Gawain, Louise L. Hay, Kutira & Raphael, Don
     Miguel Ruiz, and Ananda Sarita.

to our parents: Betty & Bill Matejka and Gardenia & Arthur Loya.

to our Ancestors. Bless and praise Tibetan Yoginis: Yeshe Tsogyal
     and Machig Lapdron.

to Osho and sannyasins worldwide.

to Amma, for introducing us.

to our plant teachers. Thank you Mayantuyacu and Temple of the
     Way of Light in Peru.

to Hrana Janto for her inspiring images of the Goddess in all her
     guises.

to Anandamayi Ma, Grandmother Elda, Pam Gordon, Lynn
     Grabhorn, Catherine Ponder, Swami Radha, Luisah Teish,
     Viramo, and Susun S. Weed.

to our supportive family . . . Hannah Aurora & Raul, Danita, Jamara
     & Jonah, Lisa, Charis & Jeremy, Mimi & Roman, Casey & Dan,
     Rosalea & David, Grandmother Barbara, Mama C., Moga,
     Elizabeth, Mazie, Parnell, Paul, Kimmie, Sarat, and Yamaya.

to Elizabeth Calvin, and all who support her, at Human Rights Watch
     for introducing Fair Sentencing for Youth to California.

to our patient wise loving guides at Balboa Press.

Contents

Introduction

"May you be joyful
May your good fortune
and happiness increase."
Buddhist prayer

This book is an offering of healing for all those who courageously choose to take responsibility for their sexual disease. Here is spiritual guidance regarding our Sacred Sexual Self. We intend to expand your sexual awareness.

We wrote this book to create peace, after years of grieving the lack of sexual joy here on our abundant Earth Mother. We offer all the opportunity to heal the tragic imbalance, which deeply affects us all, that oppressing the Universal Divine Mother has resulted in. We are guided by the Divine Feminine to share these teachings for the greatest good, for all those who are sexually exploited. Our intention is to empower you. When we treat our dis-ease with loving kindness and compassion, when we are willing to change old patterns, when we are willing to forgive; we heal our whole being.

We love sex: sex connected with love and spirit.
This is a magnificent gift.

". . . It is impossible
for us to learn elsewhere
what we are incapable
of learning within our own bodies."
Mantak Chia

We are an unique couple who have been connecting spiritually, emotionally, and sexually for eight years. During this transforming time, we have courageously opened to each other to heal our Sacred Sexual Selves. We have spent our lives contemplating our own sexual dis-eases and the global crisis.

Our spiritual journey began when Adam received the address to write to Circle of Love Inside for guidance. This is a compassionate seva created by the great Saint, Amritanandamayi Ma. Adam was surviving his life in the dire circumstances of a youth unjustly imprisoned, year number 12. He was sentenced to life locked in cage after cement steel cage, for a crime he did not commit. He was a victim of human rights violations in California. He was ready for love.

"I love how you have given me
the power to heal,
to take back my Sacred Sexual Self
and reclaim what is mine."
Turtle

This is the shaman's path: experiencing the depths. Adam is a miraculous survivor, with a very strong spirit, who is now willing to help others to heal. Adam has always had a devoted spiritual practice. He is an impassioned Mestizo artisto. He has had time to write, meditate, and cultivate. He is willing to change and eager to learn new ways of being. He values his inner child and has faced his pain to heal his wounded little boy. He also has the nurturing ability and heart-felt compassion to heal Dawnee's wounded little girl. This is of great benefit for healing our Sacred Sexual Self. Our wounded inner child can cause havoc in intimate relationships.

Adam introduced Dawnee to Toltec Wisdom. We both have ample opportunity to practice the agreement to not take things personally. Ometeotl.

Adam is a compassionate comfort to those around him. He genuinely honours, respects, and remembers the Goddess, which is very refreshing. He is truly a Divine Love God.

Dawnee introduced him to Tantra and Taoism. She joyfully shared her practice of healing herself metaphysically with Louise L. Hay's affirmations. Shakti Gawain guided us with her workbook to trust our ability to creatively visualize. Devoted Raw Chefs from around the world teach us about Blissful Food.

Dawnee is a healing artist who has practiced massage, journal writing, sacred dance, meditation, yoga, organic gardening, and inner child healing for decades on the peaceful Gulf Islands of BC, Canada. She was guided to embrace the Divine Mother in her early 20's. She loves to prepare alive food, nourishing all in the very best ways. She encourages breathe meditation awareness. Her dentist is amazed that she does not need medication to have her teeth worked on. She has always been a passionate humanitarian, speaking up for ending racism, sexism, exploitation, animal cruelty, and child abuse. She has creatively expressed her Sacred Sexual Self, as she has been guided to by Divine Love.

We fell in love in a hopeless place. We opened to love and healing no matter what. Mystical love magnetized us. Our practices of romantic love and cultivation sustain us. Faith and compassion guide us. We pray daily and create clear intentions.

We humbly share with you our pilgrimage to heal our Sacred Sexual Selves.

*"Be the change
you wish to see."*
Ghandi

**We offer you affirmations, prayers, and creative
visualizations to replace dis-ease.**

When you practice them
along with the 3 Keys of Tantra:
breathe, movement, and sound,
you create release,
and receive nurturing support from within.
We offer them to you with love and devotion for All.
May we open our hearts compassionately
to our Sacred Sexual Selves.
Every blessing of Divine Love.

"Journeys bring power and love back into your life.
If you are unable to go somewhere,
move in the passageways of the self.
They are like shafts of light,
Always changing,
and you change
when you explore them."
Rumi

". . . ultimately
you can incorporate creative visualization
as part of your natural way
of thinking and living,
moment by moment."
Shakti Gawain

Our Sacred Sexual Self— All That We Are

*"It is crucial to understand
the sacred dimensions of sex."*
Margot Anand

Our Sacred Sexual Self includes:

A physical body—our spirit's temple here on earth.
Our bodies need expression and exercise through movement.
Bodies need to be nourished by breathing deeply, filling every
cell with life-enhancing oxygen. Your body is perfectly divine
and holy as s/he is right now: at any age, weight, height, colour,
ability, and sexual orientation. Our whole body is sexually
responsive—our skin being our largest sexual organ. Our
bodies need alive organic food to optimally nourish them.

A spiritual body.
Our spirit needs nourishment too. Our spirit needs us to
breathe deeply to connect with all that we can be. Spirit needs
us to balance Goddess (our inner self or receptivity) with our
God (our outer self or assertive creative self-expression). Spirit
needs us to recognize and commit to our truth; and to express
it passionately and compassionately.

An emotional body.
We express our emotions with our voices, our sounds. Our
feelings are an essential part of ourselves, which are liberated
by releasing with sighing, chanting, toning, singing, crying,
laughing, giggling, and creative vocal expression during
lovemaking.

1

An energetic body . . .
our chakra system and aura, which are full of bright whirling colours—all the colours of the rainbow.

A sexual body,
rooted in the pubococygeus (PC) muscle, the most powerful creative muscle in our bodies. When we ground our sexual source energy, we connect with all that we are and can be. We can do this simply by tightening and loosening our PC muscle. When we are unaware and ungrounded, our sexual energy is easily exploited by others. This is our source energy centre: the creative womb in the Divine Feminine and the creative seed in the Divine Masculine. Here is the energy of mystical union and ultimate bliss.

Our genitals are referred to as: Yoni (Divine Feminine) and Vajra (Divine Masculine), names that honour our most intimate body parts.

Our Sacred Sexual Self deserves our loving approval, acceptance, attention, and creative expression. We are immensely expanded when we take 100% responsibility for our Sacred Sexual Self. Sexual union, within or with another, connecting sex with love and spirit, compassionately heals our wounds.

"Sensual and sexual energy
coursing through us unimpeded
by fears and social conditions
can cleanse the emotions
and free our life expressions
to ever greater heights and clarity."
Kutira & Raphael

"Go into sex innocently.
Go into sex meditatively.
It is a prayer.
It is one of the most sacred things,
the holiest of the holy.
It is through sex that life arrives.
It is through sex that you can penetrate
into the very source of life.
If you go deep into sex,
you find the Divine"
Osho

What is Sexual Well-being?

"Rejoice in your sexuality.
It is normal and natural for you.
Appreciate the pleasures your body gives you.
It is safe for you
to enjoy your body."
Louise L. Hay

Sexual well-being means including all of
ourselves in our sexual self-expression.
It means connecting sex with love and spirit.

To honour our Sacred Sexual Self, we create a safe sacred space to express our sexuality, our creativity, our source energy. We do this as a spiritual practice. We do this with devotion. We commit ourselves to healing our past, our guilt, and our shame; and recreating a new sexual consciousness.

To express our sexual awareness, we learn new communication skills, which respect our sacred sexuality, and that of all others. We always ask another before we enter their bodies. We talk about what we want to enjoy with each other sexually, and listen attentively. We are able to say "no" whenever we want to, and to hear "no" graciously, letting go and flowing on. We include an affectionate "afterplay" with sexual self expression.

We respectfully detach ourselves from all exploitation of others sexually. We speak up when we hear other's being sexually denigrated. We are aware that the Divine Feminine has been oppressed and exploited. We balance yin with yang within us.

We open our hearts compassionately to accept and allow all spiritual traditions to teach us.

We heal ourselves emotionally, creating a joyful self-loving life where we see others as divine light beings, no matter what they look like.

We feed our body temples the very best foods for us, acknowledging and listening to our body's guidance.

We stay focused in the now, realizing that the past is over. There is nothing we can do about it. We can create our greatest good right now. We ground our worthiness to receive sexual satisfaction and fulfillment. We maintain a peaceful mind, and a compassionate heart full of love and appreciation for the beautiful earth that is providing so generously for us all. We are willing to share with all others. We value our freedom and our expansiveness.

"Excuses begone"
Wayne Dyer

What is Sexual Dis-ease?

"Now look at the whole thing—
what nonsense we have done!
Repressing sex,
we have repressed breathing—
and breathing is the only bridge
between you and the whole."
Osho

Sexual dis-ease is when the energy
of sexual arousal is stuck in
"power-over" instead of "power-with".
Here, sacred source energy is blocked
in the power chakra (solar plexus) and
resistant to moving into the heart chakra
to create a loving sexual experience.

Sexual dis-ease includes: date rape, marital rape, incest, unwanted sexual touching, unwanted use of objects during sex, harassment, molestation, fondling, and sexual cruelty.

It also includes physical abuse, since our Sacred Sexual Self includes all of us: starving, hitting, slapping, punching, shoving, choking, smothering, cutting, stabbing, physical restraint, burning, abandoning, locking out, hair pulling, locking in a room or a cage, destroying property.

It also includes emotional abuse: threats of violence, yelling, cursing, controlling, name calling, withdrawal as punishment, forbidding contact with family and friends, refusal to socialize, manipulation with lies, telling anti-gender jokes or making demeaning remarks about your gender, criticizing sexual self-expression, minimizing feelings, lies about sexual actions.

It also includes spiritual abuse: pressure to adopt other's beliefs, lack of respect for all spiritual traditions, hatred of religions, denial of the Divine Feminine, forced celibacy, put-downs of other's spiritual practices, religious harassment, destroying spiritual customs and creations.

"It can be a joyous experience
as you lift the burden of old negative beliefs
and release them
back to the nothingness
from whence they came."
Louise L. Hay

"Now the time has come for us
to recognize this invisible thread woven
into our lives,
this common thread that
runs from our earliest foremothers to us,
this thread of love and nurturing
which can lead us out of
the maze of planetary destruction,
war, and self-hatred."
Susun S. Weed

Affirmations, Prayers, and Creative Visualizations

"Healing is an art
whereby what is diseased
is returned to its natural state of well-being.
. *Healing always empowers,*
encouraging our consciousness to take responsibility
for the well-being of the whole."
Brenda Davies

Here we have the antidote spiritually for sexual dis-ease,
enhancing our true selves, our love, and our wholeness.
Affirmations, prayers, and creative visualizations
encourage and support you in all ways.
A daily practice is best, along with a
regular spiritual practice.
Feel free to change any words to ones that work best for you,
miraculous unique you.

"We live in our bodies.
We have thoughts and identities,
relationship and emotional patterns.
We tend to think of the patterns in our bodies
and the patterns of our lives as permanent forms,
and each one,
from our deepest cells to the vastness
of our creative capacity.
is a dynamic expression that can evolve and change, . . ."
Tami Lynn Kent

Abandonment

Do Not Abandon Yourself!

A: I commit myself to loving me no matter what. It is safe for me to love myself whole-heartedly. I choose to feel secure being me. I trust my own inner guidance. I am safe in my own body. I am loved.

P: Divine Mother/Father, I thank you and honour your wisdom. Grandmothers and Grandfathers, thank you my ancestors for guiding me to this place. Help me to stay safe and grounded with your love. Help me to forgive the past. Bless and praise all that I am now.

CrV: Breathe deeply, releasing all tensions with tones and sighs. Drop your jaw as you release your anxieties. Move your body to express your feelings. Forgive all those who have abandoned you. Forgive them all easily and effortlessly now. Imagine yourself receiving all that you need and are so very worthy of. Appreciate yourself in all ways. Imagine the future that you would love to create for yourself now. Are you willing to change? What do you need to change? How do you feel when you do not abandon yourself? Accept peace and joy now. Allow for new ways of being. Surrender to receiving the best for you now. Feel gratitude for what you do have.

"Today I shape my own destiny."
Louise L. Hay

Addiction to Ejaculation

*"The curious paradox is
that when I accept myself just as I am,
then I can change."*
Carl Rogers

A: I am capable of loving. I am worthy of the best. I am willing to change. I deserve the most amazing expansive sexually satisfying experiences now.

P: Divine Love, guide me in releasing all tensions and fears of divine ecstasy, my birthright. Help me to balance my sacred sexual self-expression. Help me to experience the joys of creative love-making. Bless and praise my courageous choice to change now.

CrV: Breathe deeply and stay focused on your breath. Relax and release with movements and sound. Let go of the past and old patterns of arousal. Forgive yourself wholeheartedly. See yourself clearly taking time for lovemaking and accepting the moment to moment feelings that arise in you. Bring your aroused energy up to your heart and breath in your love. Fill your lungs and your heart with compassion and joy. Bring your energy up up up to your third eye and see yourself clearly creating the love life that you so desire. Fill your vision with clear pure indigo light. Feel gratitude, acceptance, well-being, and fulfillment as you recreate anew. Focus on your breathing and stay in the now. There is nowhere to rush off to.

Addiction to sexually exploiting other human beings

". . . loving intent is enough to heal ourselves and the entire planet."
Pi Vallaraza

A: I am willing to change now. I am ready to create a healthy sexual practice for myself now. I am proud of my Sacred Sexual Self. I take the very best care of me now. I forgive myself for wounding others and myself.

P: Loving Compassion, guide me to commit myself to healing. Guide me in seeking my own inner wisdom and peace. Guide me in forgiving myself and all others. Help me to face myself and to change now. Guide me to honour the Goddess now.

CrV: Breathe deeply and release with tones. Let go . . . and disconnect from the past. Be here right now and focus on your breathe. Move your body temple to let go! Breathe into your heart chakra in your chest. Deep breaths . . . feel the comfort and support that you give yourself with simply a deep breathe. Forgive yourself for sexually exploiting or pimping other human beings. Forgive all those who have done the same to you. Keep breathing deeply and let go of these old behaviours and beliefs. Imagine that you are in a temple now humbly on your knees. Smell the incense. Hear the chanting. Reclaim your innocence. Breathe deeply into your purity now, releasing all guilt and shame to the past. Drop your jaw and release into a whole new holy way of being which focuses on respect for yourself and all others. See yourself praying to the Divine Mother for compassionate unconditional love. Feel yourself receiving Her generous love and forgiveness. Recreate your life anew. Imagine how you feel about yourself. Express your genuine gratitude.

*"Compassion is the flowering of consciousness.
It is passion released of all darkness,
it is passion freed from all bondage,
it is passion purified from all poison."*
Osho

Addiction to Pornography

*"The pornosphere has emerged
from the shadows of the patriarchal underground
into a vast highly visible
global network."*
Brian McNair

Divine Feminine: glossy magazines which promote
the sexual objectification of the female body;
romance novels/soap operas which severely
limit a woman's self-perception.

*"Today, our women are like zombies,
like attractive caricatures of true women."*
Andre Van Lysebeth

A: I am the perfect size and shape for me now. I proudly love and accept my unique expression of the Goddess. I am now willing to change my perceptions of myself. I am now choosing the best for me. It is safe for me to reclaim my power now.

P: Wisdom Goddesses guide me to embrace my worthiness. Help me to accept the immense joy that is here for me now. Guide me in self-realization. Help me to release all oppressive old patterns and lies. Bless and praise all that I am: humble and magnificent.

CrV: Breathe deeply and delete all old messages about your size and shape. Giggle a bit about how absurd it all is . . . Breathe deeply and release with sound. Forgive all those who exploit your Sacred Sexual Self. Forgive yourself for limiting yourself. Breathe in your willingness to change now. Move to express this transforming energy now. Imagine yourself now with a daily spiritual practice which includes all that you desire to nurture your spirit and balance your emotional life. See yourself being creative in all your favourite ways. How does your body feel now? Immerse yourself in those feelings. Saturate yourself—mind, body, and soul. Allow yourself to express yourself. Accept your self-expression unconditionally. Surrender to your spiritual path. Give thanks for your ability to heal yourself.

Divine Masculine: images of others which are covertly or overtly violent or violating; always power-over and denigrating, and devoid of love.

*". . . something that once was fun
was having unexpected side effects . . .
it's an interesting feedback loop . . ."*
Pamela Paul

A: I am capable of creating loving nurturing relationships with others. I am willing to change. I let go of old patterns. It is safe for me to heal myself now.

P: Divine Mother/Father, help me to change. Guide me into the light of Divine Love. Guide me to respect children and women, taking care of them in the very best ways. Help me to forgive myself. Help me to realize your unconditional love and forgiveness.

CrV: Breathe deeply and let go of cultural norms and pressures. Release all the images of violation and denigration. Open your heart genuinely to respect other human beings. Keep breathing deeply and releasing with tones . . . let go of your pain, your shame, your guilt, and your lies. Express yourself with movement to release. Are you willing to change your power-over patterns to power-sharing? Imagine that you focus your sexual source energy on a daily spiritual practice which nourishes you. Imagine that you are using your creative energy to create just what you love. How are you feeling as you expand your consciousness? How are you feeling as you are creative? Breathe deeply and saturate your whole being with this awareness. Forgive yourself. Forgive all others for exploiting you. Forgiveness is easy. Imagine healthy sexual practices. What is on your mind now? How does your body feel? Check in with your overall emotional well-being. How does your Sacred Sexual Self feel now? Express your gratitude to all who guide you in sacred sexual practices.

"Our biological urges
need to be understood
and liberated
from the shackles of ignorance and unconsciousness."
tantra-essence

Anxiety

"Laugh as much as you can.
By this all rigid knots in your body are loosened.
You see how the laughter
that flows from your heart
lightens the world."
Anandamayi Ma

A: I am willing to relax and enjoy my life now. I am willing to release all old patterns which prevent me from receiving the best life for me now. It is safe for me to change now. I love to relax and let go.

P: Divine Mother/Father, help me to transform. Hear my sincere plea to change my life now. Help me to accept my sexuality as a natural loving aspect of me. Help me to relax and receive all the pleasure that I so richly deserve.

CrV: In a relaxed meditative mood, take a few deep breaths. Drop your jaw, releasing all anxieties with laughter and dancing. Imagine yourself the way you want to be. See yourself clearly acting in calm self-assured ways. Hear the change in your tone of voice. Taste well-being on your tongue. Listen to relaxing sounds. Feel your whole energetic being releasing old core patterns of relating. Breathe deeply, release with tones or sighs. Remember being a teenager. Forgive all others and yourself now. Remember your intimacy experiences as a child. Forgive all others and yourself now. Take time to recreate. Feel gratitude for your new relaxed way of being.

Belly Hatred

*"Every thought
you think
is creating your future."*
Louise L. Hay

A: It is now safe for me to love all of myself. I am now joyfully loving and accepting my soft roundness. I am perfect just the way I am. My belly is a natural normal part of my beautiful body temple.

P: Baubo and Buddha, help me to laugh deeply from my belly. Help me to release all fears and self-judgments. Guide me to disconnect from the dis-eased "abs" obsession of our culture.

CrV: Breathe deeply into your powerful belly bowl. No need to hold it in. Let go! Let go all old blocks and fears stored in your sacred hara. Drop your jaw and release all patterns of self-denial with sound. Move your body and release all emotional repression. Give yourself permission to love yourself exactly as you are now. Relax and breathe deeply into your clear orange second chakra. Forgive all others now for oppressing your body. Forgive yourself. Forgive the belly hating culture that we live in. Feel your heart opening with tenderness for you as you continue to breathe deeply into your body and let go in the flow. Allow and welcome change. Imagine the changes you would love in your life. See them clearly. Hear these changes. Accept these changes for the greatest good. Accept your belly and all the power that she contains. Know your worthiness to receive all good now. Give thanks for your health and well-being.

*"Women are
the greatest untapped natural resource
in the world."*
Mama Gena

Betrayal

*"Trust that life brings into being
just what is needed for your growth."*
Margot Anand

A: I am alone and choosing to feel my emotions. I am safe. I am held in the arms of Universal Mother Love.

P: Air, Fire, Water, and Earth guide me in expressing my truth. Guide me in breathing deeply, letting go in the flow, and staying focused. To those above, my spirit guides, thank you for being here comforting me. To those below, Ancestors, thank you for bringing me to this place of growth. Bless and praise all that I am: transforming energy.

CrV: Breathe deeply and let go vocally with emotion! Keep focused on your breathe to come out of shock. Know your worthiness to receive all the comfort and support you need. Move to express your pain. Imagine that the Divine Mother is nourishing you now. Feel yourself vulnerable and needy like a small baby held in Her nurturing arms. Allow yourself to receive Her tender compassionate care. Breathe it in. Breathe out your pain and forgive. Drop your jaw and forgive all others. Forgive and let go. Sing a song of praise for your ability to heal yourself now. You deserve to be protected and heard. You deserve to express your emotions. Feel gratitude for your own perfection.

Birthing Trauma

*"The quality of life
is defined
by the quality of birth."*
Elena Vladimirova

A: I now reclaim my Sacred Sexual Self. I am willing to take responsibility for my past. It is safe for me to change now. I am worthy of the very best.

P: Divine Love, guide me to surrender. Help me to make the best choices for me now. Guide me in knowing my worthiness to receive the best healing support. May all benefit.

CrV: Breathe deeply and forgive yourself for your fears. Release the past with sighs of relief. Drop your jaw as you exhale. Move your body to assert your well-being now. Imagine yourself recreating the ecstatic birthing experience that you desire. See yourself consciously choosing and receiving all the support you need. Who is there for you? Where are you? What are the colours? What sounds do you hear? What is it that you need most? Open to creating a safe healthy joy-filled birthing experience for yourself now. Imagine a sensuous orgasmic birth. Accept that you can have this. Face your fears. Allow yourself to feel the feelings of empowerment. Surrender to an ecstatic birth. Express your gratitude to all who encourage you to heal your Sacred Sexual Self.

*"The more connected you are,
the better sex is,
the better birth is,
the better life is."*
Sheila Kamara Hay

23

Blame

*"Take responsibility to make new agreements
with those you love.
If an agreement doesn't work,
change that agreement.
Use your imagination to explore the possibilities."*
Don Miguel Ruiz

A: I am now willing to create a healthy joyful life. I respect my Sacred Sexual Self. I am whole, complete, balanced, and compassionate. I am willing to change and take 100% responsibility for being me. I am an amazing empowered being creating my reality thought by thought. It is safe for me to change now.

P: Ometeotl! Help me to face myself. Guide me in expanding my compassion. Help me to forgive all those who have hurt me.

CrV: Breathe in the beauty of the day. Release all blame with sounds expressing your wounding. Breathe in and take responsibility for your pain. Gently drop your jaw and let go. Move, dance, jump! Imagine yourself clearly forgiving all who have wounded you. Let them go with love. Feel the spaciousness in your heart as you do this. What are you making way for? What are you opening up to as you let go of this emotional armouring? Keep breathing compassionately into your own heart, awakening your heart's desires. Imagine allowing yourself to receive all that you desire and are so very worthy of. How does this feel? See yourself clearly receiving all that your heart desires. Stay focused on your love for yourself. Accept yourself whole-heartedly. Surrender to your love. Express your gratitude for this transformation.

Blatantly Negative Messages

"Just as we are grateful for our blessings,
so we can be grateful for
the blessings of others."
Buddhist prayer

A: I am now removing every negative thought and belief in my mind. I joyfully embrace my Sacred Sexual Self, no matter what. I am now creatively channeling my source energy. I choose to commit myself to healing.

P: Shakti/Shiva, guide me in recreating a sex positive world. Help me to focus on love. Help me to stay tuned into the joyful rhythm of my life. Bless and praise me as I create anew.

CrV: Breathe deeply and feel joy enter your being with the simple act of breathing. Drop your jaw and release your attachments to nasty negative thought forms. Let go of repetitive old patterns with sounds. Let go of pursuits. Let go of competition. Let go of misery. Let go of oppression. Let go of exploitation. Let go of anger. Let go of depression. Let go with your breath and your sounds. Let go with movements. Forgive the past. It is all over now. Forgive yourself for not living up to your ideals of perfect. Laugh a little. Cry a little. Imagine that you are feeling joyful and ecstatic. Allow yourself to feel like this for longer and longer periods of time. Accept your joy. There is truly nothing to complain about! Breathe in this new reality of ecstasy. Feel it with all your heart and soul. Feel it in your sacred source energy centre. Connect with the Divine Mother Earth by pulsing your PC muscle. Surrender to balance now. Express your gratitude for this opportunity to transcend the past.

*"I like to imagine that I am letting go
of old beliefs
by dropping them into a river,
and they gently drift downstream
and dissolve and disappear,
never to return again."*
Louise L. Hay

Codependence

A: I am now consciously allowing myself to give the very best to me. I am now living my life for me. I now treat myself with utmost fondness. My heart is overflowing with love for me.

P: Mother/Father guide me in humbly realizing my deservingness. Help me to speak my truth for the greatest good. Help me to know my inherent worthiness. Guide me to reclaim my Sacred Sexual Self.

CrV: Breathe deeply and open up to your oneness with All That Is. Drop your jaw, releasing your old patterns with sounds. Move your body temple to release all old stuck patterns, especially in your joints. Release the past and all self-sabotaging choices. Open to new healthy choices. Forgive yourself and all others. Imagine your life now as you would love to be living it. Where are you? What are you doing in the morning? What food are you choosing? What kind of exercise are you getting? What do you do with your evenings? How are you sleeping? What do you smell? What are the colours around you now? Recreate for you. Immerse yourself in the feelings that these visions create in you. Give thanks for all that you are now.

*"To forgive is an
act of love,
an act of union . . ."*
Don Miguel Ruiz

Denial

"The stream of well-being
is always flowing throughout you.
The more you allow it,
the better you feel.
The more you resist it, the worse you feel."
Esther & Jerry Hicks

A: I am now willing to admit the truth of my life. I courageously embrace all that I am, the dark and the light, my shadow and my divinity. The truth sets me free. I am safe and I am loved.

P: Beloved Spirit Guides, thank you for guiding me to honest surrender. Ancestors, thank you for my life, at this place, at this time. Guide me, my Beloved Self, to open to my Divine Love light.

CrV: Breathe deeply into your belly, filling your lungs with rejuvenating air. Feel your whole body awakening. Release all resistance with breathe and sounds. Drop your jaw. Move your body to open up! Forgive the past. Forgive yourself whole-heartedly. Imagine that you are living a life that you love. How does this feel? What does it look like? This is for your greatest good. Choose the best for yourself now. What is it that you really want? Breathe into your heart and look within. Let go of other's expectations. Bring your love up to your visionary centre. Enhance your visions with your love. Connect with your source energy. Connect with your joy. Connect with your well-being. Courageously let go of the past and give thanks for the now.

Depression/Low Libido

"This is probably one of the most amazing tools
that you could be given,
the ability to just let things go,
not to be caught in the grip of your
own angry thoughts . . .
or depressed thoughts."
Pema Chodron

A: It is now safe for me to embrace my Sacred Sexual Self. My sexual energy is my creative source energy. This is my own energy to create a life that I love with. I now joyfully release all that does not nourish and sustain me.

P: Ometeotl! Balance the pain from my past. Help me to let go in the flow, recreating aliveness for me now. Bless and praise my abundant sacred source energy.

CrV: Breathe deeply into your wonderful nourishing lungs, filling them with sacred air. Look within for your depression. Release it now with each and every breathe you take. Release with tones and sighs, expressing your feelings now. Drop your jaw and release completely on your out breathe. Get up and move your body however you feel to. Forgive yourself kind-heartedly now. Forgive all others. Imagine your life as you would love to be living it. See yourself vividly living this perfect life for you. Imagine yourself energized! Imagine yourself feeding your body temple alive fresh food. Imagine yourself giving yourself the perfect exercise for you now. Imagine peace and well-being. Imagine abundance and joy. Open up to creating a blissful life. Expand and explore. Allow and accept pleasure. Give thanks for this lifetime of challenges.

"Each obstacle you overcome
is a stepping stone on your path to greatness.
Appreciate the obstacle,
for it empowers you
to courageously face future barriers
in your quest for success."
Tavis Smiley

Fear of Aging

"However, negative conditions
are nothing more
than the result of our own
past focus . . .
and feelings and energy flow."
Lynn Grabhorn

A: I trust the river of life. I accept and allow the natural flow of my life. It is safe for me to surrender to blissful well-being at any age. I am loved. I am now much more loving.

P: Guide me, Divine Love, as I lovingly embrace my ageing. Help me to accept my new wrinkles and sags, and to have a sense of humour about it all. Guide me to take responsibility for being a Beloved Elder now.

CrV: Take a deep breathe, filling your all three lobes of your lungs with rejuvenating air. Release all judgements and fears with your out breathe. Drop your jaw and drop off all old images of yourself. Dance to express yourself now, at any age. Forgive the ageist culture that we live in and the exploitation of our body temples. Allow yourself to be all that you can be now.

Imagine that you are facing your 60's now. How would you love to be living? What would you love to be doing? What colours do you see in your future? Who are you with? What are you doing?

What about your 70's? See yourself clearly living your greatest good. What do you smell? What do you eat? How do you exercise? What changes are you making during this decade?

Move into your 80's . . . where are you now during these years of your joyful life? What exercise do you do now? Any changes in what you eat? What are the colours of your life now?

And the 90's . . . where are you now? How are you being loved and supported? How are you facing and creating your death? Give abundant thanks for this amazing life on Planet Earth. Sing Hallelujah!

"No mud,
No lotus."
Tantric proverb

Fear of Arousal

"In its fullest meaning,
sex is
beautiful beyond compare."
Catherine Ponder

A: I now choose to be aware of my arousal. I love and accept all that my Sacred Sexual Self is aroused by. It is safe for me to express my arousal in creative loving ways. I am worthy of Divine Bliss.

P: Shakti/Shiva guide me in honouring all that you are within me, this miraculous being that I am. Help me to connect my sexual energy with love and pleasure. Help me to know and honour my oneness with All. Help me to know my holiness.

CrV: Breathe deeply, releasing all tensions with sound. Drop your jaw. Breathe deeply into your chest. Acknowledge your fears and let them go. Look at your childhood, your programming, and your beliefs which have created these fears. Gently and compassionately continue to release them now with the perfect movements for you. Forgive others for all eternity. Forgive yourself. Keep taking full breaths, filling your belly. Release the past. Imagine yourself now as a sensual aroused being all day every day, rhythmically allowing waves of ecstasy to enrich your life. Allow sexual well-being. Accept your sexual needs. Surrender to your Sacred Sexual Self to guide you into the mystical mysteries of sex. Give thanks for your divine body temple who creates these blissful feelings.

Fear of Intercourse

"Sexual Union is a door
provided by nature
to access
an ecstatic state of being."
Sarita

A: It is now safe for me to receive sexual pleasure. This is my birthright! I can say "no" whenever I want to. I am safe. I am now completely willing to surrender to ultimate ecstasy.

P: Divine Mother/Father, guide me in expressing my sacred sexuality. Help me to relax and be all that I can be here now. Help me to love and enjoy my body fully. Help me to connect sex with love and spirit.

CrV: Breathe deeply. Surrender your past to forgiveness now. Forgive yourself always. Drop your jaw and continue to breathe deeply, releasing all fears with your voice. Allow yourself to express your feelings now. Move to release all that blocks you. Clear your vision centre by flowing some pure unconditional love for yourself into your third eye with crystal clear indigo light. See yourself receiving all that you need to relax and experience intercourse now. Feel good feelings replacing all fears now. Feel your joy with this loving experience of oneness with your Beloved. Imagine your ecstasy! Feel your sense of fulfillment. Surrender to persistent pleasure. Imagine yourself receiving all the "afterplay" love and support that you need. Give thanks to the spirit that sustains you.

Fear of Orgasm

". . . orgasm is a nutrient
that has been missing from the
standard human diet
for centuries."
Nicole Daedone

A: I am willing to surrender to receiving abundantly for me now, all that I deserve and desire. I am now compassionately opening my heart to me. I allow myself to receive pleasure. I give to myself joyfully and generously.

P: Shakti/Shiva guide me as I feel my exquisite empowered life energy flow. Guide me in receiving the deep satisfying sexual bliss that is your Divine Feminine expression. May my joy and fulfillment radiate to all.

CrV: Breathe deeply. Release all the tensions of the past by dropping your jaw. Express yourself with your voice. Loosen up! Look within your heart to face your fears. Let them go, flowing in a river of love. Compassionately forgive yourself. Forgive all others. Laugh. Giggle. Imagine yourself relaxing into orgasmic ecstasy. This is a natural normal healthy experience. Feel your ultimate joy and fulfillment. Pulse your PC muscle and awaken your awareness of your sacred source energy. Ground all your visions in the divine Earth Mother. Allow yourself to receive generously for the greatest good. Accept your worthiness to receive now. Surrender to bliss. Feel your gratitude for orgasmic pleasure.

"Sexual orgasm gives you
the first glimpse of meditation . . ."
Osho

Fear of Self-loving/Cultivation

*"The damage caused to human society
by the condemnation of sex
is incalculable."*
Margot Anand

A: I am now surrendering to loving my Sacred Sexual Self. I am celebrating my creative source energy. I am accepting my sexual needs as a normal natural healthy part of life. It is safe for me to love myself now.

P: Love Goddesses and Gods, help me to realize my deep joy being sexually alive and aware. Help me to let go of all old patterns of self-abuse. Help me to relax into receiving my deepest needs. Guide me to love myself and reclaim my Sacred Sexual Self.

CrV:. Breathe deeply into your belly bowl. Face and release all old beliefs that you have about self-loving or cultivating your sexual energy. Release by dropping your jaw. Release with movements and with sounds. Let go of your guilt. Let go of your shame. Let go of old wounds. Forgive the past. Forgive yourself unconditionally. Imagine that you are creating a safe sacred space to self-love in now. What does it look like? How does it smell? What images do you have around you? Do you have a playful prayerful attitude? Spend time appreciating and honouring your sacred body temple. Massage your whole body as you pray. Become aware of your sexual energy at this time. Tune into your needs. Give to yourself. Love yourself joyfully, ecstatically, and freely. Breathe deeply and express yourself. Surrender. How are you feeling now? Feel this feeling from the tips of your toes to out the top of your head. Give thanks for your Sacred Sexual Self.

Fear of Spirituality

*"By banning the awareness of our transcendent nature
and the healing powers of the sacred feminine
and spiritual wisdom in general,
our culture deprives us of our true selves,
our true hearts,
and our true wholeness."*
Andrew Harvey

A: It is now safe for me to explore my spiritual self-expression. I trust my guidance and open to the vast array of spiritual practices that are here for me to choose from. I embrace my Sacred Sexual Self joyously. I love to connect sex with spirit.

P: Divine Love, guide me on my spiritual journey. Guide me to connect my sex with love and spirit. Help me to know my sacredness. Help me to release all spiritual oppression.

CrV: Relax as you enter safe sacred space now. Ground your source energy by pulsing your PC muscle. Breathe deeply and drop your jaw. Release your fears with movements and sounds. Imagine a clear pure white light all around you now. This Divine Love light is supporting and encouraging you to be all that you are spiritually. Breathe deeply and see yourself clearly praying in ways that nourish your own unique spirit. Hear the sounds of your spiritual practice. Smell the smells. You now have all the support you need to express yourself spiritually for the greatest good. Breathe in these new awarenesses. Face all fears that come to meet you. Open your heart to yourself. Forgive all others. Forgive the past. Most generously, forgive yourself. Feel gratitude for your freedom now.

". . . the work required to ensure
that you live up to
your highest potential and greatest good
is sacred inner work
and conscious outer work."
Iyanla Vanzant

Frigidity

"The sexual ecstasy of a woman has a very high value.
It is a magical healing force.
When she has been well loved, sexually
fulfilled, she herself becomes a Goddess
with magical powers . . .
she has the capacity to restore the life force of sex
to its rightful place
in the opening the way for planetary
healing and transformation."
Margot Anand

A: It is now safe for me to love and nurture my Sacred Sexual Self. I love my body. I love my yoni. I love being alive! Orgasms are a healthy!

P: Divine Love, help me to realize my worthiness to receive divine ecstasy. Help me to forgive generously and compassionately. Guide me in opening my heart to receive my divine birthright—sexual bliss.

CrV: Relax in safe sacred space and feel pleasant well-being. Become aware of your breathe. Form a clear vision of yourself enjoying sexual pleasure like never before. Keep breathing through all the blocks and resistance. Let go by dropping your jaw and releasing with tones or sighs, singing or crying, raging or chanting. Let go and move your body temple! Feel yourself supported and encouraged by All That Is to release all of your self-denial and self-sabotage now. Allow images of your past as a youth to come and pass on, fading away. Forgive all these old patterns. Forgive yourself most readily. Accept your Sacred Sexual Self. Surrender with joy. Feel abundant gratitude flood your whole energy system now. Feel your oneness with all of life.

Genital Mutilation

"To love means to open ourselves
to the negative as well as the positive—
to grief, sorrow, and disappointment
as well as to
joy, fulfillment, and intensity of consciousness
we did not know was possible before."
Rollo May

A: I am now willing to release the past. I am reclaiming my Sacred Sexual Self from all who violated me. I reclaim my purity from all who defile me. I am worthy of a blissful Divine Feminine body temple now. It is safe for me to care for and honour my Sacred Sexual Self.

P: Divine Mother/Father, help me to forgive all those who lied to me. Help me to accept my vulva now and care for her in the very best ways. Guide me in receiving pleasure, for this is my birthright. Help me to expand and explore my pleasure potential.

CrV: Breathe deeply into your belly bowl. Release the pain of the past by dropping your jaw. Express your pain with your voice. Express your grief. Express your rage by moving your body. Express your sadness. Forgive all others and cultural traditions. Release them now. You are free and they are free. Imagine that you are encouraged and supported to be a healthy vibrant radiant empowered Goddess now. What does this feel like? Image your life in vivid indigo light. What do you smell? Where do you feel safe? Where do you feel free? Allow yourself to feel these peaceful feelings. Accept that you deserve to live your life here on earth like this: safe and free. Expand upon what this looks like for you. Sing a song of joy to enhance your vision. Stay focused on your pleasure now. Give thanks for your ability to heal your Sacred Sexual Self.

> *". . . if you really love*
> *your women and children . . ."*
> Fatoumata Diawara

Grief

"You become
what you think about."
Wayne Dyer

A: I am now willing to feel my feelings and express them in creative ways. It is safe for me to feel my pain and sadness; my anger and confusion. I now take time for myself to meditate and pray.

P: Ometeotl. Guide me in recovering my balance. Help me to let go, Divine Spirit, trusting that all is well. Help me to express my feelings, without silencing or shame. Help me to let go.

CrV: Breathe deeply, connecting with your own sacred breathe. Fill your belly, your hara, your emotional centre with life-affirming breathe, and let go. Drop your jaw and release all that is unlike love. Forgive yourself as you explore the unfathomable world of grief. Forgive all others whole-heartedly. Stay in touch with your pain and release it with sound. Dance to express yourself. Write to express yourself. Create to express yourself. Imagine that you have all the support and encouragement you need to express your grief now. All of your grief. What does this look like for you? What does it feel like? What do you smell? What colours do you see? What is your heart expressing? Feel yourself supported and encouraged by the unconditionally loving Divine Universal Mother. Feel Her comfort and concern for your well-being. Accept Her love. Allow Her love. Surrender to Her nourishment. Express your humble gratitude.

Guilt

"Sex is life . . .
sex energy keeps you alive.
Drop the foolish ideas that you have been taught.
This has been done to many people in different ways.
A thousand and one inhibitions and
taboos have been created."
Osho

A: I love and accept my Sacred Sexual Self. This is a natural authentic part of me. I allow myself to heal my past to create sex positive ways of being. It is safe for me to change now.

P: All That Is, guide me in releasing all past pressures to oppress my sexuality. Help me to reclaim my purity. Help me to own my energy for me, creating the very best for myself now, honouring and respecting my Sacred Sexual Self.

CrV: Breathe deeply and expand your awareness of who you are. You are worthy to receive the best life. You are worthy to receive all good. You are worthy to receive new ways of living. Drop your jaw and drop off all your guilt now with sounds. Forgive yourself for guilt-tripping. Forgive others for instilling guilt. Imagine yourself as an innocent child. Feel your joy. Feel your curiosity. Feel your playfulness. Immerse yourself in these feelings. Cleanse yourself of your past. Become child-like again. Move like a child. Explore your life with openness. Give thanks for this wonderful adventure.

Heartbreak

"The reason why love and compassion
bring the greatest happiness is simply that
our nature cherishes them above all else.
The need for love lies
at the very foundation of human existence.
It results from the profound interdependence
we all share with one another."
The Dalai Lama

A: It is now safe for me to love myself unconditionally and compassionately. I choose to let go of the past and recreate the best for me. I am free to create my life the way I desire it to be. All of creation supports me.

P: Thank you Divine Love, for breaking my heart open. I am humble before you. Guide me in reclaiming my love. Help me to transform, changing myself in the best ways. Bless and praise all that I am opening to now.

CrV: Breathe deeply into your heart chakra now. Express your emotions with movement and sound. Drop your jaw and release. Release your rage. Release your pain. Release your clinging. Forgive all others. Forgive yourself unconditionally. Focus on you now. Imagine yourself receiving the very best nurturing. What are the comforts that you truly need now? What foods do you choose to nourish yourself with? What exercises are best for you now? What scents do you smell? Who do you call on? Where do you feel safe? What are your new boundaries? Accept transformation. Allow change. Express gratitude for this challenge.

Homophobia

A: I am now joyfully balancing my yin and yang energies. I am relaxing and accepting lesbian and gay lifestyle choices. I am willing to accept my own sexual needs. It is safe for me to be compassionate now.

P: Divine Love, guide me in accepting my dualities. Guide my inner male to listen to the Goddess within and serve Her devotedly. Help me to realize my oneness. Guide me in courageously being all that I can be. Help me to honour and respect all Sacred Sexual Selves.

CrV: Breathe deeply and release old prejudices. Face your fears one by one, releasing them with breath, movement, and sound. Expand your awareness to the realm of choices always available to us all. Forgive all who have wounded you. Forgive yourself always. Imagine that you are born accepting your Divine Feminine and your Divine Masculine selves. Imagine that you are accepted exactly as you are, unique wondrous you. Feel your worthiness to be all that you are here on the beloved Earth Mother. You deserve to be here exactly as you are. Feel secure in your own sacred sexual self-expression. Feel gratitude for all your blessings of this lifetime.

Impotence

"The obsessive sexualization
of almost every aspect of our culture
has made us all
profoundly insecure."
Andrew Harvey

A: It is now safe for me to be a virile male. I relax and enjoy my Sacred Sexual Self. Expressing my sexuality is a sacrament. I am innocent. I am loving, loveable, and loved.

P: Shakti/Shiva guide me in loving and accepting my Sacred Sexual Self now. Help me to release all old negative patterns. Guide me in accepting my vajra and his self-expression. Help me to let go of the past. Bless and praise my sacred sexuality now.

CrV: Breathe deeply, relax your jaw as you exhale, and take 100% responsibility for your sacred body temple now. Release all resistance to change. Release all those stuck old pattens with sound and movement. Release power-over patterns. Release competition. Release self-denial. Release self-sabotage. Forgive yourself. Love yourself. Imagine expressing your sexual energy in the very best ways now, for the greatest good. Image a healthy lifestyle, including alive food and your favourite exercises. How do you feel? Allow yourself to feel joy. Open up to your own inner ecstasy. Pulsate your root and feel good. Expand your awareness of all that sex can be. Prolong your pleasure. Give thanks for this great blessing of mystical sex.

Incest

*"Consider your body as
a living temple of the divine
supported by Mother Earth
who holds
all sustainable resources
for life itself."*
Kutira and Raphael

A: I admit the truth. I am willing to release all guilt and shame now. I forgive and release the past.

I now speak my truth with ease and clarity. I reclaim all of my sacred source energy for me now.

P: Beloved Spirit Guides, thank you for opening up a past door to face my wounded Sacred Sexual Self. Help me to gently close this door now, with love and gratitude for all the teachings of this forbidden love. Help me to accept my confused feelings of pleasure and pain. Guide me to let go with love. Help me to detach from all shame and blame. Help me to release all judgements of this taboo. Comfort the child within me who was not heard, Divine Mother.

CrV: Take a deep breathe and go inward to that dark place within you where you were taken advantage of and hurt deeply. Forgive all those who hurt you. Breathe deeply, letting go with tones and dropping your jaw. Breathe deeply and soften your heart. Open your heart compassionately to the child within you who was exploited and violated. Love this child unconditionally. It was not their fault. Dance a healing dance for yourself. Imagine receiving all the comfort and support that you have always wanted and needed to heal these

47

wounds. Cleanse yourself of all guilt and shame now for all eternity. Breathe deeply and see yourself clearly receiving all that you deserve to heal from this trauma now. How does this feel for you? How does it smell? What colours are around you? What are you tasting? Keep breathing deeply and releasing all connections with being powerless. Reclaim all of your vital life energy now. Neutralize the past. Release all negative memories in a river of love. Acknowledge your safety now. Express your gratitude for your freedom and peace.

> *"I release you now to your highest good.*
> *I love you and I release you*
> *to complete freedom and complete health,*
> *in whatever way is best.*
> *I am free and you are free."*
> Catherine Ponder

Injustice

"Imagine
one billion women
releasing their stories,
dancing and speaking out
at the places where they need justice,
where they need to end violence
against women and girls.
Rise! Release! Dance!"
Eve Eisler

A: I am 100% worthy of all the best that the universe has to offer. I am most worthy now and have always been. I never did deserve to be treated unjustly. It is safe for me to change now.

P: Oh Divine Creator/Creatress, guide me in opening my heart to receive justice for me now. Help me to release my past life of suffering. Help me to know my worthiness to receive the very best for me now.

CrV: Breathe in justice! Fill your belly with rejuvenating air and release all injustice with sounds and movements now. Drop your jaw, releasing all unfairness now. Generously forgive all wrongdoing. Feel free inside and out. Imagine that you are given justice now. What does this look like for you? Imagine yourself receiving all the pleasure and joy that you are so worthy of in this life. Expand your visions. What colours do you see? What do you smell? What sounds do you hear? What are your diet and exercise choices? Stretch and feel your freedom now. Laugh and enjoy refreshing justness. Allow yourself to feel safe feeling pleasure. Accept your birthright. Surrender to these new ways of being. Express gratitude for justice now.

Internalized Oppression

"Miracles now follow miracles
and wonders never cease
to manifest
as the divine plan of my life."
Catherine Ponder

A: I am now loving and accepting my body as my sacred temple. I am joyfully expressing myself creatively. I am expanding my awareness of sexuality and all that it is for me. It is natural to experience sex connected to love and spirit. It is safe for me to support and encourage my Sacred Sexual Self.

P: Ancestors! Guide me in releasing all old patterns that are unlike love. Teach me to humbly love and accept myself unconditionally. Help me to surrender to oneness with all that is here for me now. Guide me in releasing all those who have oppressed me.

CrV: Breathe deeply and release all old beliefs about power-over. Release them all simply with tones and sighs. Drop your jaw. Move your body to release pent up emotions. Breathe deeply and let go. Let go of all internalized oppression held in your beautiful body temple. Forgive all who oppress you. Breathe deeply and release them all to their greatest good. Let them all go. It is all over now. Let go of societal expectations of you. Let go of all emotional oppression. Let go of all spiritual oppression. Let go of all sexual oppression. Imagine that you are free to be all that you were born to be now. What are you creating? Who are you with? What are you nurturing yourself with? What are your greatest pleasures? Give yourself all that you desire here now. How are you feeling about yourself and your life now? Express gratitude for your amazing body temple and the healing power of breathe.

"There are so many negative viewpoints
surrounding pleasure, . . .
pleasure is actually of the utmost importance
because it is the connective tissue
between a woman and her own life force."
Mama Gena

Jealousy

*"Always practice what
your heart says."*
Luisah Teish

A: Thank you for showing me what I desire, my feelings. It is now safe for me to provide abundantly for myself. I forgive myself for denying myself all that I desire. I let go, and let love guide me.

P: Divine Love, guide me in expressing my greatest good now. Help me to be the best that I can be here on earth now. Help me to surrender to the guidance of my deepest emotions. Guide me in expressing the magnificence of my light!

CrV: Breathe deeply and surrender to your breathe. This is your connection with life. Drop off all the tensions in your jaw. Release them all with sound. Open your fifth chakra to express your pain. Image a clear blue light flowing through your throat chakra. Express your anger with movements and your voice. Express your jealousy! Let it out and let it go. Kindly forgive yourself. Forgive all others. Imagine that you are allowing yourself to receive what triggers your heart's desire. See it clearly and vividly. How do you feel, now that you have what you need? Expand your joyful feelings. Accept this new way of being for yourself. Be patient. How are you preparing for your dreams come true? Give abundant thanks for this prolific universe that we live in.

Lack of Boundaries

"Open your eyes wide!
Look! See the world before you.
Close your eyes.
Breathe! And see the light within you."
Luisah Teish

A: I am grounding and owning my all of my energy for me now. I am aware of and responsive to my needs. I am now safely providing for myself all that I desire. I can say "no" whenever I want to. I love and protect me now.

P: Ometeotl, guide me in honouring my Sacred Sexual Self. Help me to know my worthiness to receive for me. Help me to share all that I am in the very best ways. Help me to respect my precious unique self-expression.

CrV: Breathe deeply and relax your jaw, releasing with your voice. Let go of old patterns of care taking others. Forgive yourself for not valuing yourself. Forgive all others for using you. Imagine that you are now free to live your life as you choose to. What changes would you make? Who would you say "no" to? How would you protect yourself? What new guidelines would you live by? How would you love yourself more? See yourself moving freely in your new way of being. Accept all the support you need to make changes. Allow yourself the joy that you are so very worthy of. Surrender with gratitude to these transformations as they lead you to Divine Love light. Give abundant thanks for all the pleasure you are worthy of.

Lack of Remorse

". . . invoke the Mother of the Universe.
Worship the Divine Mother
with your whole heart,
and she removes every difficulty."
Linda Johnsen

A: It is now safe for me to feel compassion. I open my heart to express my remorse to all those who I have violated. I am sorry to create pain instead of love. I am willing to change now. I choose to create loving kindness.

P: Mother of the Universe, guide me with your unconditional love to release all old negative patterns. Help me to face my darkness and reclaim my light. Forgive me, compassionate Divine Love, for my mistakes.

CrV: Breathe deeply into your belly bowl and release with movements and sounds. Drop your jaw. Feel connected with All That Is. Breathe into your heart chakra, awakening with your breathe. Forgive yourself fully now, opening your heart compassionately to you. Forgive all others, releasing them now to their greatest good. See yourself as a youth. How were you treated? Were you sexually disrespected in any ways? Breathe through your own pain. And release the past. It is all over now. Imagine that you are now able to create all the love and honouring that you have lacked in your precious life. What does this life feel like? How are you feeling about yourself now? What are the colours around you? What do you hear? What spiritual practice is guiding you? What food do you choose to eat? How do you exercise your body temple? Give thanks for your miraculous ability to heal.

Lies

*"Be aware
of the quality of your communication.
It depends on whether
you tune your emotional body
into love or to fear."*
Don Miguel Ruiz

A: It is now safe for me to speak my truth. I now clear my heart of all lies. I am willing to change. I feel a radiant glow from within when I speak my truth.

P: Ometeotl. Guide me in facing the truth of who I am. Help me to honour my truth. Guide me to speak my truth.

CrV: Breathe deeply into the core of your being. Release all resistance to releasing your lies with your voice. Drop your jaw and move your body. Close your eyes and look at all your sexual lies within. Release them one by one with your breathe and your voice, relaxing and releasing into the authentic you. Forgive yourself for lying now. Forgive all others who have lied to you sexually. Forgive the whole world, full of sexual lies. Imagine the honest loving sexual lifestyle that your spirit longs for. How are you expressing yourself now? What are you saying? What are you feeding your body and spirit with? How are you feeling about your love life? What sounds are you listening to? Is your body temple exercised and hydrated? What colours to you see? Give thanks for your new life of freedom to be honest about who you are.

Loneliness

A: I now realize my aloneness. I embrace it as my very nature. This is my reality.

P: Toltecayotl, give me the strength to become aware of my aloneness so that I am not a stranger to myself. Help me to value my uniqueness. Guide me in loving myself always in all ways.

CrV: Breathe deeply and release your fears of facing the truth of human existence. Drop your jaw, releasing with sounds and movements all obstacles in your way. Imagine that you are feeling healthy and whole just as you are. Feel secure being alone with you. Smell the scent of you. Look into your eyes and smile. Look into your heart and embrace balance. Know your worthiness to receive the blessings of the Divine Mother/Father. Surrender to the pleasure of your existence. Express gratitude for this fountain of abundance within you.

Misogyny

"Tantric precepts are . . .
it is considered a violation
to disparage women in any way,
especially to denigrate their spiritual qualities
or the purity of their bodies."
Judith Simmer-Brown

A: I am now courageously embracing my Divine Feminine. I am supporting and encouraging all others to honour their inner wisdom. I am one with my wholeness and well-being, balanced yin and yang. It is safe for me to receive love and guidance from the Mother of the Universe now.

P: All That Is, guide me in loving acceptance of all that I am. Help me to compassionately integrate my Divine Feminine, my Goddess energy, honouring and respecting Her in all ways. Guide me in releasing all denial, repression, fears, and resistance so that I may know oneness, joy, and peace. Guide me in connecting with Mother Nature and Father Sky.

CrV: Breathe deeply and release all old tensions from your belly, solar plexus, and heart chakra. Use your voice to release all old emotional baggage that you are carrying around. Shake it off. Shake your shoulders and let it go. Let go of old beliefs and stuck patterns of dis-eased thinking. Let go for your well-being. Shake your arms and hands. Shake your legs and feet. Wiggle your toes. Shake your head and let it all go. Imagine that you have always known that there is a Divine Mother who stands beside the Divine Father. Expand your awareness to realize all the Goddesses who are here to help you always. Accept this receptive part of you. Imagine an infinity symbol in your sixth chakra, your third eye, balancing all that you are. Envision in indigo light. This results in a more balanced world. Pledge your willingness to change dis-eased ways of thinking and acting. Express your gratitude for yin energy.

"We believe that in this century
the paramount moral challenge is . . .
gender equality around the world."
Nicholas D. Kristof & Sheryl WuDunn

Neglect

"Harmonious sexual relations
are possible only
when the man makes love with the attitude
that serving female satisfaction
is his first and foremost goal.
The battle of the sexes would suddenly stop
if men surrendered in this way."
Ellen & David Ramsdale

A: I am willing to connect with my creative life source energy, my Sacred Sexual Self, now. I joyfully connect sex with love and spirit. It is safe for me to receive all the loving attention that I need. I deserve pleasure!

P: Forgive me, Divine Love, for denying and oppressing myself. Guide me in honouring your sacred teachings. Help me to express my balanced Sacred Sexual Self. Bless and praise Shakti/Shiva within me.

CrV: Breathe deeply and fill your heart and lungs with awareness of how healing pleasure can be. Feel your own joy and ecstasy. Release with your voice all that blocks your joyous self-expression. Move to express your life energy. Imagine yourself receiving all that you desire in a sexual connection with your Beloved. Imagine yourself giving all that you wish to. Imagine a flow of giving and receiving, naturally joyful and playful. Imagine giving from your heart. Imagine your intentions. Imagine all benefiting from your choices. Forgive the past. Forgive all others. Always forgive yourself for neglecting your needs. Give thanks for this opportunity to nurture yourself.

"Divine Love,
expressing through me,
now draws to me
all that is needed to make
my life complete."
Catherine Ponder

Premature Ejaculation

"The sexual imbalance between
men and women is obvious."
Mantak Chia

A: I am willing to slow down and relax, taking time to be here now. I release all performance pressures. I surrender to Divine Bliss. It is safe for me to express my love. I love to connect sex with spirit.

P: Love Gods guide me in allowing the virile male that I am to express myself with loving creativity. Help me to heal my past. Help me to change. I am willing now. Guide me in allowing myself a fulfilling sexual life.

CrV: Breathe deeply and take 100% responsibility for your body temple now. You can heal. Release all tensions in your body by feeling it and letting go . . . drop your jaw and let go with your voice. Let go with vigorous movements. Go inward and feel your heart wounds. Release them now with forgiveness for all eternity. Forgive yourself deeply and completely. Honour your sacred vajra and his self-expression. Release all hatred and oppression now. Imagine that your body is healthy. What are you eating to create this well-being? How are you exercising your body temple? Do you have a daily spiritual practice? How are you expressing your creativity? Are you experiencing your joy? Are you smiling? What new ways of thinking are you practicing? Express your gratitude for this amazing opportunity to transform, guided by yourself, wonderful wise you.

"Cure illness
with stillness.
Meditate daily."
Luisah Teish

Rage

*"Giving thanks reduces anger,
transforms greed,
and purifies lust."*
Christopher Hansard

A: It is now safe for me to be a spiritual sexual being. I am willing to let go of the past and recreate a culture of love. I radiate love to all now.

P: Pele, Volcano Goddess, help me to release my rage in safe ways. Help me to release all guilt, all shame, and all blame. Guide me in opening my heart to Divine Love now. I am safe. I am free.

CrV: Breathe deeply and imagine a volcano of your raging fury moving up your spine from your sacrum. Drop your jaw, releasing your rage with sounds as you move this cleansing potent energy up your spine and out the top of your head. Breathe and release. Breathe and release. Move your pelvis and release all your genitalia's rage. Move your belly bowl and release your hara's rage. Breathe deeply into your solar plexus and release your resistance to reclaiming your power now. Feel your heart expanding as you gently release all the anger armouring your love. Release with sound any last frustrations and bring this clear pure creative source energy up to your indigo eye and image change. Transform your life. Recreate anew. Connect with the oneness of All That Is, releasing pure violet light out the top of your head. And give thanks for purifying your sacred source energy.

Rape Offender

*"The only thing
constant in the world
is change . . ."*
india.arie

A: I am capable of changing now. I forgive myself for cruelly violating others. I choose to be kind hearted and thoughtful. I consciously release the past and begin anew.

P: I ask the Supreme Powers within me to heal me now. Help me to control myself. Guide me to realize the sacredness of my sexuality. Help me to forgive myself.

CrV: Breathe deeply into your pain and release it with your voice. Drop your jaw, and release your violating past. Move your body temple in a cathartic release. Throw out all of the junk! Forgive yourself deeply and completely. It is all over now. Imagine that you are now able to create a loving safe sacred sexual relationship. What does this look like for you? How does it feel? What spiritual practice is guiding you? Envision how you are taking care of your body now. What are you eating? How are you exercising? Accept all good coming to you now. Allow yourself the peace to transform. Surrender to new ways of being. Give thanks for this chance to change your consciousness.

*"Everyone needs healing,
because healing is simply
about balancing."*
Sarita

Rape Victim

*"If you wait until you become perfect
before you love yourself,
you'll waste your whole life.
You're already perfect right here, right now."*
Louise L. Hay

A: I am wholly holy. I never did deserve to be treated like this. I deserve respect and honouring always. It is now safe for me to recover from violation. It is now safe for me to let go and move on.

All is well.

P: Help me, Divine Love, to love myself unconditionally. Guide me to receive all the support I need to heal. Help me to know my worthiness to receive the best that life has to offer. Guide me to open my heart to receive compassionately for me now.

CrV: Breathe deeply as you release your pain with your voice. Drop your jaw and release all guilt, shame, and oppression. Dance to your favourite music. Reclaim your power now. Reclaim your own genitalia and/or mouth. Reclaim your vision of your life. Forgive all those who have violated your Sacred Sexual Self. Remember your joy. Imagine that you are receiving all the support and encouragement that you need to recover now. What does this look like? Feel your well-being and your power to heal yourself. Feel protected and respected. Feel all the love that you need being offered to you now. Remember how precious you are. See yourself protected with Divine Love light. See yourself choosing healthy foods and lovingly exercising your body. Image a daily spiritual practice that nourishes your spirit. Reclaim all good for yourself. Express your gratitude for your resilience and courage to heal yourself now.

"I am created by divine light
I am sustained by divine light
I am protected by divine light
I am surrounded by divine light
I am ever growing into divine light."
Swami Radha

Recovery from being prostituted

*"Whether a woman sacrifices her
soul for a classy marriage,
is a swinging single
or engages in prostitution,
she is acting out of the mistaken belief that sex is the way
to secure what she needs."*
Charlotte Kasl

A: I am now worthy of my own self-love. I deserve to be safe and protected. I am now courageously creating a new life for me. I deserve the best. I accept the best now.

P: Divine Love, guide me in self-acceptance. Help me to forgive myself and all that I have been. Guide me in recreating anew. Bless and praise my unlimited creative potential and my ability to heal the past.

CrV: Take a deep breathe and reclaim all of your sacred source energy for you. Your body is sacred. Your body temple is holy. You deserve respect and honouring always. Release the past with your voice. Allow yourself to express your pain with movements. Feel your breathe rejuvenating your body. You are worthy. Genuinely forgive yourself now. Face your oppressors one by one and compassionately release them. Let go, dropping your jaw as you release. Imagine a wonderful new life. Break through all boundaries now. You are worthy of the best. What is best for you now? What does your new life look like? How does it smell? What do you taste? See the earth that you walk upon. See abundant prosperity. See creativity, fulfillment, and safety. Breathe in deeply and know your worthiness. Know your beauty and preciousness. Open your heart to creating the best for you now. Ground these visions in the Divine Earth Mother. Pray to your spirit guides. Listen to spiritual music. Express abundant gratitude for your recovery now.

*"This fusion of male and female (regardless
of actual gender) is holy . . .
Great pain is caused by misplaced
or misused sexual desire."*
Tami Lynn Kent

Recovery from being Stalked

"We are the only ones
responsible for our beliefs
about our worth."
M. Rogers & T. Tamborra

A: I am safe now. I now release all anxieties and fears into the past. I free myself of past restraints. I love my life.

P: Divine Mother/Father, guide me to relax and know my safety. Help me to create joy in my life. Guide me to awaken to true love and genuine caring.

CrV: Breathe deeply releasing all tensions with tones and sighs. Drop your jaw as you release the past. Express yourself! Move! Breathe deeply into your heart and forgive. Forgive others and free yourself. Forgive yourself in all ways. Imagine yourself living in a safe sacred space where you are honoured and supported. What does this look like for you? How does it feel? What are the colours? What do you smell? What are the sounds? Breathe in this refreshing new lifestyle for you now. Accept your ability to create peace for yourself now. Allow yourself to release the past, letting go of all of your suffering. Surrender with gratitude to this blessed new way of being.

Recovery from Being Trafficked

"I seek support so I
can let go to my depths."
Susun S. Weed

A: I never did deserve to be treated like this. I am safe now.
I am free. I am worthy. I am now recovering completely. I let
go of the past and move on, recreating the best for me now. I
reclaim my Sacred Sexual Self for me now.

P: Divine Love, help me to forgive all those who have violated
my human rights. Help me to know my worthiness to receive
peace and safety now. Guide me, Divine Mother/Father to
make the best choices for nurturing myself now.

CrV: Breathe deeply and release with sounds all that you
have survived. Keep breathing deeply into your belly bowl,
relaxing. Release your oppression with lively movements.
Release all your abusers. Image facing each and every one
and releasing them from your energy system with forgiveness.
Forgive yourself. Reclaim all of your energy for you, wonderful
precious worthy you. No more brutality and lies. Envision
your new life. See yourself protected and secure. You can say
no whenever you want to. Feel yourself moving spontaneously
whenever you feel to. Dance your freedom dance. Sing your
freedom songs. Chant your freedom chants. Immerse your
visions in pure indigo light and know your worthiness to
receive now. Feel your freedom vividly and give thanks.

"Act as if anything you desire is already here.
Believe that all that you seek
you have already received,
that it exists in spirit,
and know that your desires are now fulfilled."
Wayne Dyer

Romantic Dysfunction

*"Wholeness is all that goes into
how we live our lives . . .
Wholeness is
how we dance the dance of life."*
Amy Sophia Marashinsky

A: It is now safe for me to be open hearted and tender. I now give myself permission to express and explore my romantic passions. I am creating the best romantic self-expression daily now. I am truly blessed.

P: Goddesses of Love, guide me in surrendering to feelings of joy, tenderness, and bliss. Help me to balance my Divine Feminine with my Divine Masculine. Help me to open my whole being to all the blessings of love. Guide me to surrender to pleasure.

CrV: Breathe deeply and let go with sound. Dance to express your passion. Release all tensions. Release all fears. Release all old limitations. Forgive all others and let go of all bitterness now. Forgive yourself tenderly and compassionately. Imagine yourself now living an abundant life, full of joy and well being. What does this life look like? Where are you? What do you hear? What do you give to yourself when you deserve all good? You are now free to let go of your past and recreate romance for you. Surrender to your romantic inclinations now. Give thanks for this opportunity to expand your pleasure potential.

Self-loathing

"Care for your body.
Self-love and self-acceptance
are the ultimate acts of self-care."
Cheryl Richardson

A: I love and accept myself whole-heartedly now. I am perfect just the way that I am. I rejoice in the way I am. It is safe for me to love myself now.

P: Divine Mother/Father. Help me to become one with my worthiness now. Guide me in letting go of the past and making all the changes that I need to create the best love life for me now. Open my heart to know my beauty and joy. I am truly deserving, Divine Love. Show me the way.

CrV: Take a deep breathe and release all that is unlike love in your attitude towards yourself. Drop your jaw, letting go of all those old lies that you've been told with your voice as you exhale. Keep breathing deeply and dropping your jaw to release. Let go of all stuck old patterns out of all your joints with movement and light. Open your heart compassionately to you. Forgive yourself for feeling this way about you, precious worthy you. Forgive all others who conditioned you to feel this way. Release all bitterness and wounding. Imagine that you are perfect just the way that you are. Realize the incredible unique soul that you are. See your awareness flooding your body, mind, and spirit with abundant Divine Love light. Expand your consciousness to become aware of all the light all around you. Immerse yourself in healing joyful light. Express your gratitude for your amazing Sacred Sexual Self.

Separation from your Beloved

"The essence of love
is surrender."
Arthur Jeon

A: All is well. We are connected in our hearts and spirits. Nothing can come between us. Nothing can stop us from communicating however and whenever we choose to. Everything is possible in spirit.

We are safe and we are free.

P: Divine Love guide us into the light. Help us to maintain our joy, our love, our clarity, and our devotion. Guide us to surrender to allowing our love to grow. Help us to face the challenges of separation. Bless and praise our sacred journey to oneness.

CrV: Breathe deeply, drop your jaw, and release all loneliness with your voice. Allow yourself to feel your sadness. Acknowledge your longing. Accept your grief. Express your feeling with movements. Forgive all that separates you. Forgive yourself benevolently. Imagine that your Beloved is with you always. Feel the peace in your body. See your Beloved clearly with you now. Feel how good this feels for you! What are you doing together? What colours are around you? What music are you listening to? Feel the mystical joy of your oneness. Radiate this love to all. Become a fountain of love. Humbly express your gratitude for the loving pleasure that you do share.

"I want to live
with and open heart."
india.arie

Sexual Abuse

"May you be held in compassion
May you be free of pain and sorrow
May you be at peace."
Buddhist Prayer

A: I am willing to release the past, forgiving all, myself included. I accept the spiritual teachings of these experiences. I allow myself to realize my most magnificent loving self now. I embrace my Sacred Sexual Self. It is safe for me to heal now.

P: Divine Love, help me to forgive those who wounded me. I did not deserve to be treated like this. I deserve to be sexually respected and honoured. Help me to choose the best for me now. Help me to respect myself sexually. Guide me in loving myself always exactly as I am.

CrV: Deep cleansing breaths and sounds release your anguish, your pain, your grief, and your rage. Drop your jaw and let go, let go. Express yourself with movements, unrestricted and uncensored. Let go of your guilt and your shame. Open your heart to compassionately healing yourself now. Generously forgive each and every one who has disrespected your sexual integrity. Forgive them for their ignorance. Forgive them for their greed. Imagine that you are giving your Sacred Sexual Self your genuine loving attention now. What does this look like for you? What are you nourishing your body, mind, and soul with? How are you nurturing your spirit? How are you reclaiming your power? Feel the abundant support and encouragement of the Universal Mother bathing you in tender gentle Divine Love light. Immerse yourself in this infinite abundant love. You are worthy of the best. You deserve to be loved and cared for. You deserve 100% recovery from all sexual abuses. You can do it. Be patient. Keep releasing the past and forgiving all. Give thanks for your strength and well-being now.

"If you have been the victim of unwanted sexual desires . . . Take courage and gather the resources you need to assist you. You will inevitably restore your authentic desire and rediscover a source of profound nourishment and joy."
Tami Lynn Kent

Sexualization

*"The influence of pornography
on mainstream culture is certainly substantial,
part of that wider set of trends
often referred to as
cultural sexualization."*
Brian McNair

A: I am free to reclaim my innocence and purity. I now embrace my Sacred Sexual Self. I desire to express myself wholly. I am willing to change my beliefs about sex now.

P: Toltecayotl, guide me to balance. Help me to understand the reality of my Sacred Sexual Self.

Guide me to release all that is unlike love. Help me to open to my unique spirit's guidance.

CrV: Take a deep breathe, filling your lungs with rejuvenating air. Drop your jaw as you release the past with movement and sound. Take time to release all the trash polluting your mind and being. Forgive all who have sexualized you. Forgive the pornographic culture that we live in. Forgive yourself for your ignorance of your Sacred Sexual Self and your needs. Imagine that you are immersing yourself in safe sacred space. What does this look like for you? How are you feeling? What do you smell? How are you relating to others in different ways? How are you changing your actions? Allow yourself to embrace your sacred spirit. Accept new ways of being. Surrender to the very best for you now. Express your sincere gratitude for this joyful transformation.

*"Sexuality, emotions,
creativity, and intuition
all play a role in healing."*
Sarita

Sexually Transmitted Dis-eases

"Love is the only thing that matters.
Sex
is the most intimate
and empowering
way to express Love."
Christa Schulte

A: It is now safe to express my greatest creative potential. I am aware of and responsible for my sacred sexual energy. I open my heart to connect sex with spirit. I am one with Divine Love always.

P: Infinite Love, guide me in releasing all the wounding of my Sacred Sexual Self. Help me to transform into the radiant light being that I am here to be. Bless and praise all that I am right now.

CrV: Breathe deeply and release all guilt, shame, and pain with sounds. Drop your jaw and let go of the past. Keep letting go of old patterns and old programming. Forgive yourself and all others. Release with your breathe and moving your body temple. Imagine that you are free of all anxiety. Imagine what a healthy life looks like for you. How are you feeling? What are you eating? Do you have a daily spiritual practice? How do you feel about your sexually active self? See yourself clearly transforming your sex life now. Smell the change in your own body. Hear new sounds. Accept that your sex is connected to your heart and to your spirit. Allow your wholeness. Surrender to the naturalness of sex. Balance your self-expression, including yin with yang. Give thanks for this opportunity to heal your dis-ease.

Sexually violating attitudes/behaviour
"Bully Sex"

"Be compassion—unconditionally,
undirected, unaddressed.
Then you become
a healing force
in this world of misery."
Osho

A: I am willing to change. I forgive myself for the past. I forgive all who taught me these disrespectful ways of being. I am free to transform now. It is now safe for me to become the very best that I can be.

P: Sacred Breathe, guide me in breathing deeply and letting go of old patterns. Water, cleanse me of my past. Fire, ignite new ways of being within me. Beloved Earth, ground me here and now. To those above, Spirit Guides, thank you for bringing me to this place. To those below, Ancestors, thank you for guiding me to change and grow. Thank you, Divine Spirit within me, for choosing the best for me now.

CrV: Breathe deeply and relax your jaw. Open up to new ways of being with your breathe. Release the past with movement and sounds. Move your sexual source energy up from your genitalia through your solar plexus and into your heart. Feel your heart soften as you release your armouring. Forgive yourself for your behaviours and beliefs. Forgive all those who taught you. Imagine that your Sacred Sexual Self has been always treated respectfully, from the day you were born. Imagine yourself as a baby, being optimally nourished and cared for. Feel your peace and well-being. Imagine yourself as a child, well-protected and innocent. Cherish this childhood. Imagine yourself as a teen, well-educated about sex and given permission to naturally explore your sexuality. Imagine that you were always respected sexually. See what this looks like for you. Laugh at the ridiculousness of these old patterns. Accept that you are willing to change now. Allow yourself transformation time. Surrender to ultimate unknown pleasures. Express your gratitude with loving kindness.

> *"The master key*
> *to all healing*
> *is love."*
> Sarita

Shame

"Live in joy . . .
Live in your innermost nature
with absolute acceptance
of whosoever you are."
Osho

A: I am now free to embrace my wholeness. I am willing to release all that is unlike love. I love and accept myself 100%. Nothing can stop me. I know my worthiness to receive and give pleasure. I connect sex with love and spirit. It is safe for me to love myself now.

P: All those who guide me! Help me to release my past. Help me to forgive myself and all others who have shamed my Sacred Sexual Self. Guide me in knowing my worthiness to receive all the support I need to heal myself now. All Knowing Ones, I surrender to your guidance now.

CrV: Breathe deeply and release all your shame now, over and over with your out breathe. Forgive others for shaming you. Forgive yourself for being ashamed. Breathe deeply and release with tones, sighs, movements, and dropping your jaw. Let go of all old restrictions and oppression of your Sacred Sexual Self. Image that you have always been innocent as a baby. Reclaim your innocence and purity now. Feel compassion for your Sacred Sexual Self who has been so cruelly oppressed. Remember your worthiness to receive the best for yourself now. You are a beloved spirit. You are unique. You deserve all good. Give thanks for this joyful transformation.

"Easy is right."
Zhuangzi

Shock

". . . let go of fears
and swim in that river of life . . .
It requires determination,
wisdom, courage, and above all,
the willingness to change."
Pi Vallaraza

A: I am here now, grounded and clear. I am safe. It is safe for me to change now. I trust change.

P: Divine Mother/Father help me to heal my wounds. Guide me to release the past and let go. Help me to receive the compassion that I am so very worthy of. Help me to express my wisdom and courage.

CrV: Breathe deeply, drop your jaw, and let go with tones expressing your feelings. Forgive all others. Forgive yourself whole-heartedly. Move and let go! Keep breathing deeply into your lungs and ground your sacred source energy, reconnecting with the Divine Mother. Image a new you, recovering from your shock. What do you look like? What are you doing? Where do you live? What do you smell? Imagine a balanced life where time for meditation and prayer is valued. See yourself with a satisfying daily spiritual practice. See yourself choosing to feed yourself a healthy diet. See yourself exercising in the very best ways for you. Give thanks for your willingness to change now.

Stress

*"Life give us so much opportunity
to work spiritually."*
Tenzin Wangyal Rinpoche

A: I am one with the unfolding of my life. I breathe deeply and consciously every breathe I take. I am willing to change my lifestyle to create peace. I am calm and relaxed. I am joyful and creative now.

P: Ometeotl. Guide me to release all my tensions and worries. Help me to know my worthiness to receive a pleasureful life now. Help me to change! Help me to grow! Help me to create health and well-being!

CrV: Breathe into your belly bowl and release with sighs of relief. Simply let go with your exhalation. Drop your jaw, letting go of old patterns of tightening-up and hanging on. Drop all war games. Drop all competitions. Drop all stresses now. Move your body and let go. Release with colour through all your chakras. Forgive your mind for creating stress. Forgive the stressful culture that we survive in. Imagine yourself living a peaceful leisurely lifestyle. What does this look like for you? What does it feel like? Feel these feelings and expand them now. Allow yourself to change your way of being. Accept pleasure and joy. Accept radiant well-being. Allow yourself to be the best that you can be now. Surrender to balance. Give thanks for this awareness of inner calm.

Teen Pregnancy

"Image, image, image . . .
all the good that you wish to experience."
Catherine Ponder

A: I accept the unexpected. I listen to my guidance. I am worthy to make my own choices. This is my life, and my sacred lessons. I surrender to my greatest good now.

P: Divine Love, All That Is, guide me today in hearing my inner guidance. Help me to surrender to the greatest good for me with this challenge. Divine Mother/Father, guide me to make the best choices for me now.

CrV: Breathe deeply, releasing on the out breathe with sound. Let go of the past and all that you have been. Relax your jaw as you gently release. Dance to release your fears. Dance to release the chaos. Dance to release other's judgements. Forgive all others, and focus on you now. Imagine that you are receiving all the help and support you need at this vulnerable time in your life. Imagine that you have all the spiritual support that you need. How are you feeling now? What are your new priorities in life? How is your life changing? What colours do you need? What food do you need? What exercise do you need now? What spiritual practice is guiding you now? Express your gratitude for all the challenges that life gives us.

Temptation

"To flow
is to know what nectar is
and to become stagnant is
to know what poison is."
Osho

A: I now let go of all repressed thoughts that create my own temptations. I clear my conscious mind as I focus on my breathe. All is well.

P: Divine Love within me, guide me to rid my consciousness of all temptations. Help me to become aware of my Divine Spirit within my body temple which knows only freedom. Help me to replace negative addictive old patterns with willingness to change. Help me to know my worthiness. Help me to know my oneness with you.

CrV: Breathe deeply and calm your mind. Breathe naturally into your belly bowl, feel your flow, and gently drop your jaw. Breathe in positive changes and breathe out repressions, releasing with sound. Breathe in your pure worthiness, breathe out temptations. Move your body to express your emotions. Forgive yourself for your past behaviours. Forgive all others who have tempted you with immorality. Image yourself living a healthy sex positive lifestyle. What does this look like for you, wonderful unique you? How are your needs being met? How are you taking care of yourself now? How do you feel about yourself? How are you expressing love in your life now? Give abundant thanks for this opportunity to love and approve of yourself.

Termination of Pregnancy

"Your pain is the opportunity
for transformation . . ."
Tenzin Wangyal Rinpoche

A: I let go with love. I am worthy. I deserve the best now. I love and accept myself no matter what.

I allow death to transform me.

P: Beloved Ancestors who brought me to this place, guide me in creating anew. Help me to take 100% responsibility for my life now. Bless the spirit who brought these precious teachings to my life. Help me to heal and release all wounding. Bless and praise my willingness to be whole.

CrV: Breathe deeply filling your belly with rejuvenating air. Release with a sighs as you drop your jaw. Keep letting go and express your grief with movements, whatever feels right for you. Forgive yourself always. Forgive all others who have wounded you. Imagine that you are being cared for now in the very best ways. Focus on your needs. What do you need now? What do you smell? What colours are around you? How do you need to eat and exercise? Accept change. Allow for your greatest good. Surrender to the teachings of this sacred time. Express gratitude for all that you have received from spirit.

Uptightness

"Ecstasy is freedom."
Osho

A: It is safe for me to relax and mellow out now. Everything is happening at just the right time. There is nothing that I need to do, and nowhere to go at this moment. I love relaxing, letting go, and going with the flow.

P: Ometeotl. Help me to relax and enjoy my life here on earth. Help me to feel my joy and connectedness with all that is here for me. Help me to trust my awakening to newness. Guide me always on my sacred path to divine bliss. Guide me to love and accept my Sacred Sexual Self.

CrV: Take a nice deep breathe deep into your belly bowl. Release with a tone, over and over. Focus on releasing tension from painful parts of your body temple as you drop your jaw. Forgive yourself for hanging on to old stuff, and let go, let go, let go. Loosen up! Move your body to release! Imagine yourself living a peaceful calm lifestyle. What does that look like for you? How does it feel? What smells do you smell? What sounds do you hear? What changes are you making? How does your belly feel? How does your heart feel? See yourself laughing. Give thanks for your ability to change—and sing joyfuly.

Unwanted Pregnancy

"Divine Love
is doing its perfect
work in this situation now,
and all is well."
Catherine Ponder

A: I am capable of facing this challenge now. I am never given more than I can handle. I tune into myself and make the best choices for me now.

P: Divine Mother/Father—guide me in this time of great need. Help me to face the darkness and move joyously into the light. Help me to listen to my heart. Help me to stay in my body, nurturing myself as I change and grow now. Help me to accept and love myself as I decide what is best for me. Help me to stay focused on my greatest good.

CrV: Breathe deeply and allow the past to flow out of you with your out breathe. Drop off all tensions by dropping your jaw with a tone or a sigh. Release the shock, release the fears, and release the past with intuitive movements. Accept the present moment and imagine yourself receiving all that your heart desires. What is it that you truly do need now? Visualize yourself clearly receiving this. How are you feeling? What are the colours around you? What sounds do you hear? What do you smell? How is your body temple feeling now? Forgive yourself for being receptive. Forgive all others and their reactions. Express gratitude for these spiritual teachings.

Vaginal Dis-ease

"The well-being of the world
needs
female sexuality and enjoyment,
relieving female sadness."
Nancy Blair

A: It is safe for me to be Divinely Feminine now. I am extraordinarily beautiful, perfect exactly as I am now. I am connected with the Divine Mother Earth who is guiding me always to express my creative receptivity. I am worthy always to create abundantly for me now.

P: Thank you Divine Love, for creating me in the image of the Divine Feminine. Help me to know my holiness. Guide me in reclaiming my empowerment as a creative energy source here now. Guide me in knowing my worthiness. Help me to forgive all that is unlike love. Bless and praise me in all ways, as I do deserve all the blessings of health and well-being.

CrV: Breathe deeply, filling all 3 lobes of your lungs with air, revitalizing air. Drop your jaw on the out breathe, and release your distress with your voice. Release your dis-ease with your breathe and with movements. Release all old vaginal wounds. Forgive yourself wholeheartedly and compassionately. Forgive all others and the sexually exploitative world that we live in. Forgive the misogyny that oppresses us. Imagine that you are healthy and free of dis-ease now. How do you feel? What does your life look like? How does your Sacred Sexual Self feel now? What colours do you see around you? What do you need to eat? What exercise does your body need now to recover? Reclaim your power to love yourself and give yourself abundant pleasure. Express joyful thanks for your healing capacities.

Workaholism

*"Follow your Bliss
and the Universe
opens doors for you
where there once
only were walls."*
Turtle

A: It is now safe for me to balance out doing with being. I intend to value my yin, giving equal time and attention to my receptivity. I feel healthy and whole living my life like this. I deserve to relax and receive pleasure. All is well.

P: Shakti/Shiva guide me to balance. Help me to reclaim my inner wisdom. Help me to know my worthiness to live a peaceful prosperous life. May all benefit.

CrV: Breathe deeply, letting go of all the tensions and demands of your life. Take some time to breathe and release, dropping your jaw as you release deeply with movement and sound. Forgive yourself. Forgive the work obsessed culture that we survive in. Imagine your life in balance. What do you need most? What do you so truly desire? Listen to the messages of your heart now. What is your soul yearning for? Vividly imagine this now. Allow yourself to receive all that your heart desires right now. See it clearly before you. Accept what your soul needs. Give generously to yourself now. You are worthy. Forgive yourself for your self denial. Express your gratitude for these inspiring visions guiding you to transform.

"Pray lovingly
Pray deeply
Pray so deeply
that the prayer and praying become one."
Deborah L. Price

Sexual Healing Meditations

*"Meditation allows you to go beyond the mind
and get in touch with spirit.
Get to know the "Unified Field"
intimately,
where true success in all fields of endeavours is possible
—instantly!"*
Deepok Chopra

Creating Safe Sacred Space

I pray to the East, asking for air's guidance to help me to breathe deeply, nourishing every cell in my body with life-enhancing oxygen.

I pray to the South, asking fire to cleanse my desires, releasing me from the past, recreating anew.

I pray to the West, asking water to help me to let go in the flow, letting go of all wounding.

I pray to the North, asking the Divine Earth Mother to ground me as I transform.

To those above, Divine Spirit Guides, thank you for bringing me to this place of bliss.

To those below, Ancestors, thank you for guiding me on our sacred life journey.

Thank you, my magnificent Divine Spirit, for choosing this sacred path to oneness.

I joyfully choose to release all negative thoughts. I am now courageously standing on my own two feet, supporting and encouraging myself. I am now generously giving myself all that I need. It is now safe for me to expand and grow. I am healing, honouring, and hearing my Divine Feminine—the Goddess within. I am balanced yin and yang, I am a joyous bright light here on planet earth. I am now allowing myself to receive all that I desire—my destiny. I am focused and clear.

Breathing deeply, I now release all that is unlike love by dropping my jaw with a tone or a sigh. I pulse my PC muscle, connecting my root with the Mother Earth. I awaken my sacred sexuality, my kundalini energy. I allow myself to feel aroused. I accept my pleasure whole-heartedly now. I surrender to my oneness with all that is. I stay connected with prayers and affirmations as I expand my sacred source energy, enlivening me! I feel my immense joy and connectedness with all that I am, owning all of me for me. I am magnificent, clear, and bright. I am wholly holy. I radiate my abundant Divine Love light to all.

"So if a negative idea comes,
immediately change it
to a positive thought.
Say no to it."
Osho

Self-Cultivation

*"You can facilitate transformation
by using imaginative journeying techniques
to get at the core
of your unconscious."*
Amy Sophia Marashinsky

Create an alter. Give yourself the gift of receptive love. Shine the divine light of love on your genitalia and reclaim your power to connect with pleasure and spiritual nourishment. As you practice this meditation, caress and arouse your body temple. Remember ecstatic moments that you have experienced. Free your wild energy, essential for your growth and fulfillment.

Create your best intention(s) for this cultivation of sacred source energy.

Ground your sacred sexual energy by connecting with the living Mother Earth. Feel your own sexual energy, your creative source energy in your first chakra. Visualize a clear deep bright red flowing down from your PC muscle into the centre of the earth. Pulse your PC muscle and connect. Reclaim all your pure innocent sacred sexual energy for you. Release all past judgements and negativities from your sacred genitalia. Contract and relax your anal sphincter muscles (external and internal). Release all rectal taboos and tensions stored here. Feel secure and well-cared for.

Breathe deeply, release with a tone or a sigh, drop your jaw, and bring your attention to your hara, your second chakra. Visualize a clear revitalizing orange flowing through this energy centre. Breathe and pulse your PC muscle, releasing all tensions, anxieties, fears, doubts, guilt, old patterns, old beliefs, limitations, and obstacles. Release all shame for feeling pleasure now. Release the past in the river of love. Reawaken feelings of rejoicing. Allow, accept, and surrender to emotional well-being.

Breathe deeply, release with sound, drop your jaw, and bring your attention to your third chakra, in your solar plexus. Own your empowerment now. Visualize a warm radiant yellow light clearing this chakra from all that prevents your from expressing your power now. Feel your power! Radiate your light! Feel your fire! Pulse your PC muscle and release all power-over energy that you no longer need. Expand in positive bliss.

Breathe deeply, release with sound, drop your jaw, and bring your attention to your fourth chakra, filling yourself up with your love for you—absolute unconditional support and encouragement for you. Visualize lush rich green filling up your heart centre. Relax your shoulders and allow yourself to release all burdens, bothersome worries, self-criticisms, excuses, lies, grief, sadness, and heartbreaks with breathe, sound, and pulsing your PC muscle. Joyfully release all self-denial now. Say out loud as many "I love yous", as passionately and genuinely as you can. Ask Divine Love to fulfill all your heart's desires. Ask and you receive, this is our connection with our creative self, our spirit.

Breathe deeply, bringing your attention to your fifth chakra. Visualize a crystal clear blue cleansing this chakra now. Drop your jaw and release all that prevents you from speaking your truth. Sing praises to yourself now. Say affirmations and prayers. Express your precious voice.

Breathe deeply and bring your awareness into your sixth chakra, your visualization centre. See a clear deep true indigo light lighting up your visions. Pulse your PC muscle and release all illusions. Envision yourself receiving all that you desire now. Ground these visions in the sacred Earth Mother by connecting with your PC pump.

Breathe your creative source energy out through the top of your head, your spirituality centre. Visualize ethereal violet light opening you to oneness with all, connecting with infinite abundance. Detach from your past and recreate! Surrender to your vision. Let go . . . let go . . . let go . . and experience your oneness with all creation.

Breathing consciously, bring your attention slowly back down through each chakra grounding yourself in your first chakra, pulsing your PC muscle, and feeling your connectedness through the bottom of your feet with the earth. Give thanks to all for your transformed awareness.

Include a significant time for "afterplay". This is an extremely potent time for affirmations, prayers, and/or feeding yourself the very best nourishing foods.

> *"Go deeper and deeper into meditation*
> *so you can go*
> *higher and higher into compassion."*
> Osho

"Sexercises"

All "sexercises" are best done
in Safe Sacred Space for the
maximum quality benefits.
Allow for a minimum of 20 minutes
each time you practice these transforming
gifts from Divine Love.
They often release emotional pain.
Please take time to rest during "afterplay".

*"imaging . . . the central nervous system
doesn't distinguish between real experience
and intensely imagined experience,
and it doesn't care where its stimulation comes from.
To image is especially valuable for women
to prepare their bodies for sexual encounter . . ."*
Saraswati & Avinasha

Cupping Genitalia

"Silence is the greatest gift."
Deva Premal

Breathe deeply and take turns placing each hand upon your own or your Beloved's genitalia. Place the other had on your heart chakra. Look lovingly into each other's eyes or close your eyes.

Alone, you may image your love god/dess.

Simply feel your feelings as you experience this blissful connection.

The Divine Mother

"The infinite love of the Divine Mother
is streaming toward us
from all sides with unprecedented power."
Ramakrishna

Breathe deeply and open your heart to the teachings of the Divine Mother.

One partner sucks the nipples of the other while being held and nurtured as a precious baby.

Alone, you may imagine yourself in as a mother giving unconditional love to her child from her heart. Focus on expanding your love. Also, imagine sucking in this nurturing mothering love.

Feel comforted and nourished.

Inner Child

*"Laughter
brings you
closest to prayer."*
Osho

Be playful. Play being children at a certain age together. Play affectionate parent-baby games.

Fulfill your wounded child's greatest needs. Laugh, giggle, be silly, sing songs, and wrestle playfully. Reclaim your original innocent state. Ask for what you want openly, like a child. Express your emotions, moment by moment.

Journal Writing/Art/Dance

Express your Sacred Sexual Self creatively! This is immensely helpful in decompressing centuries of oppression. You are able to transcend your pain and create beauty. This satisfies your soul.

Speaking your truth in the safe sacred space of your journal validates your experience.

Emoting in this safe way enables profound healing.

Writing about your sexual wounds and fantasies gets them out of you, in front of you, facing you.

Art expresses all that we are. There are so many creative mediums to choose from. Experiment and explore you and the world around you.

Dance releases as we express ourselves. There are ancient healing connections between music and dance that permeate our human experience.

> *"Divine Love*
> *is doing its perfect work*
> *in you*
> *and through you now."*
> Catherine Ponder

Orgasmic Envisioning

As you are orgasming, this is the time to affirm your visions. Say them and see them. Move your sacred source energy up to your voice and envisioning centres (5th and 6th chakras). Prolong your orgasms. Expand your pleasure potential. Clarify your visions. Put your heart into it! And release out the top of your head into Universal Oneness as you orgasm on . . . and on . . .

> *"Tantra is the*
> *art of transcendence*
> *through total expression,*
> *fearless exploration*
> *with an adventurous and innocent heart."*
> Santoshi Amor & Niten

Erotic Massage

"The body is the door,
the body is the stepping stone
to the inner consciousness—
and our body is always
in the present."
Anasha & Anubuddha

Massage is so wondrously healing combined with your Beloved's warm heart.

Begin your touch at feet of your receptive Beloved who is laying down peacefully on her back in safe sacred space. Guide your yin partner to breathe deeply, each and every breathe, and to release with a sound. Rub scented oil slowly and sensuously onto her skin, while affectionately affirming her strength and beauty.

Massage your way intuitively up her legs, asking for feedback about pressure. In the same relaxed manner, massage her genitals, including her anus and belly bowl. Guide her to breathe deeply, to relax, and to enjoy. Nurture her yoni/his vajra with your loving touch. Ask her if she would like her clitoris and/or Goddess spot massaged. Ask her if she would like her external and internal anal rings massaged. Ask him if he would like his prostate gland massaged via his anus, after his rings are relaxed. The anus is a tension zone which responds well to gentle touch. Ask him if he would like his prostate gland massaged via his PC muscle.

Continue massaging your way joyfully up his body, including kisses, licks, and love play as you move this delicious aroused energy up to his heart centre. Encourage your loved one to open up to receiving more love than ever before. Encourage him to expand his pleasure potential here now. Awaken his heart chakra with love taps, nipple sucks, tickles, and tender caresses.

Chant together, as you move this potent sexual energy up to his throat chakra. Visualize a clear blue light clarifying your truth. Guide your loved one to tone as he releases all that blocks his truth. Massage his face tenderly. Kiss his head generously. Tap his third eye and see crystal clear indigo light flowing through this chakra.

Move all his energy out the top of the head with a vigorous scalp massage, opening to Divine Love light. See violet light feeding this chakra.

Ask your Love God/dess to turn over. Massage from the top of her head down the spine to her sacrum.

Remember to keep breathing deeply and releasing all tensions. Breathe into the muscles and soften.

Breathe into the joints and clear. Breathe into your pain and let go. Massage down the backs of his legs.

End this 2 hour session at the feet of your Shakti or Shiva. With prayer, express your gratitude.

Allow for rest before activity.

Rebirthing

Here we are consciously recreating our own births.

Breathe deeply and imagine that your parents consciously conceived you during a spiritual celebration of their love.

Image them both being loving and attentive to you while you are growing in your mother's womb. Hear their loving voices. Feel their harmony and joy. Feel their loving massages.

Receive the best nourishment. Know your worthiness to receive love.

Imagine a peaceful ecstatic birth as your mother naturally trusts herself to release you to life. Your other parent is right beside her, supporting and encouraging her.

Imagine that you are welcomed with love and adoration, no matter what your sex is.

Feel loved. Know your worthiness to receive love. Love this "baby you."

> *"The core of meditation*
> *is witnessing . . .*
> *Pure witnessing, without judgements,*
> *brings us into harmony*
> *with cosmic presence . . ."*
> Sarita

Right Mindfulness

With abundant loving kindness, we release all negativity from our minds.

Dawnee has done decades of research studying the ancient teachings of Tantra from all over the world. Much to her dismay, the Goddess has been obliterated, denied, and denigrated for centuries. Many "authorities" refer to prostitution as the oldest profession. This is a lie deeply imbedded in our psyches to deny the Divine Feminine authority. Our first profession is healers, or priestesses. We were the ones who taught youth about their sacred sexuality. Girls and women have been denied access to spiritual and sexual teachings world wide. Our sacred sexuality has been prostituted. Our body temples have been sold. No one has the right to buy or sell our bodies. This is perhaps the oldest sin of mankind. Now we live in a global economy where millions of men violate children and women all over the world with complete impunity.

Adam has spent decades listening to men from all races and cultures violating and denigrating the Divine Feminine. He experiences great resistance when he introduces new loving attitudes towards the Goddess to men's awareness.

We encourage and support, along with millions of others, a conscious change of attitude by male beings, and the male in each and every one of us, who have been ruthlessly bullied into accepting these unbalanced and unhealthy beliefs. We intend to create a firm boundary protecting the Divine Feminine from further exploitation.

Breathe deeply and realize the truth of balanced equality. Drop your jaw and release all old patterns of power-over. Accept power-sharing. Allow yourself to hear your own Divine Feminine and her wise guidance. Surrender to change for the greatest good. Reclaim your sacred source energy for you. Give thanks for your ability to create a kind and loving world. Envision a world where men nurture and support women and children always, in all ways.

"We are all a magnet for miracles."
Louise L. Hay

Triangle of Bliss

Focus on igniting your sexual fire and connecting this aroused energy with your heart chakra.

If you are alone, give to yourself and/or image another giving to you.

One partner is totally receptive (yin). The other is actively loving yin's nipples and yoni or vajra in an intuitive triangle. Yang's intention is to expand yin's pleasure potential. Be aware of how much pleasure you receive from giving pleasure to your Beloved or to yourself.

Affirm your worthiness to receive all that your heart desires. Open your heart to receiving for yourself now! Breathe deeply and express your joy with movements and sounds.

Always include abundant loving attentions for the sacred lotus flower or yoni. Be gentle and patient please. She is full of energetic potential. When her clitoris, her G spot in her vagina, and her anus have been generously loved, she fountains forth bliss and well-being. Please do not pressure her for climax or penetration. Stay focused on giving to her what she needs now, nurturing her sexually. There are abundant spiritual teachings in her expansive ecstasy.

Vajra needs to receive abundant pleasures as well. His frenulum is a friendly energizer. His prostate gland loves massages via the PC muscle or anus. Explore his anus' healing needs. Encourage his full body and internal orgasms. Allow for his emotional self-expression.

Express your humble gratitude for this meditation. Relax in "afterplay.

Yab Yum

This is the ultimate spiritual meditation to satisfy our need for balance.

Yab yum may be practiced clothed or nude, by same sex or opposite sex lovers. One partner sits on top facing the other on a chair or on the floor. His varja may be inserted into her vagina in any of his states of arousal.

Focus on breathing as you look into each other's eyes, or touch foreheads or lips, or close your eyes to go inward to the light. There is no outer movement.

You may also meditate on this image/feeling/teaching on your own.

Practice, practice, practice.

*". . . touch is synonymous
with life itself."*
Anasha & Anubuddha

Blissful Food

"I discovered that
when the body, mind, and spirit
were simultaneously given all the proper nutrients,
the natural human state that I achieved
was one of bliss."
Heather Cunliffe

The most blissful food that you can choose to feed your precious body temple is organic and alive.

This is also the best food sourced from a healthy planet. Sprouted seeds are #1 freshest crunchy nourishers. Fruit, vegetables, nuts, seeds and roots are our original food sources. In their raw form, they feed us optimally.

"Living Foods:
There is a way to eat that extracts life-sustaining energy
from Mother Nature
and helps open the subtle energy bodies
to the living spirit within them."
Susan Smith Jones

We love to feed each other slowly savouring every delicious mouthful while watching our Beloved eat. We nourish our body temples during "afterplay", with love and gratitude for the best quality foods that we choose. Eating together and feeding each other creates another spiritual ritual of love. When we remember where these foods came from, the Divine Mother Earth, and give thanks, we heal Her, and ourselves. When we eat foods from sustainable sources, we are choosing well-being for all.

> *"Please always make conscious choices*
> *that positively impact your life*
> *and the lives*
> *of all the earth's creatures."*
> Megan Elizabeth

We want to open up to life by choosing fresh alive food, including abundant leafy greens. We loosen our jaws by chewing our food slowly. This also creates saliva which aids in digestion. These are new ways of nurturing and nourishing ourselves. They are cruelty-free. They do not close down our digestive system with negative impact. Raw organic foods energize us in holistic ways. They heal our Sacred Sexual Self spiritually and emotionally, in the simplest of ways.

> *"Plants are part of the web of healing,*
> *and their role is revered.*
> *Healing with plants*
> *has been an integral part of life on earth*
> *since the earliest times . . ."*
> Rosita Arvigo & Nadine Epstein

OM MANI PADME HUM

Adam and Dawnee Loya have been miraculously guided from deep within to heal our Sacred Sexual Selves. Although we are unable to express our love physically, we do experience profound orgasmic bliss. We are truly grateful for our abilities to communicate empathically.

Guided by spirit, we offer you affirmations, prayers, and creative visualizations to change past patterns. With clarity and truth, we encourage and support each and every one to accept, allow, and surrender to creative joyful ways of being. We challenge you to forgive.

It is our pleasure to share with you our favourite meditations and simple "sexercises". We are inspired to promote living foods to heal all dis-ease.

Adam is a Toltec Shaman practicing diligently while unjustly confined in a California state prison as a youth offender for the past 2 decades. He offers Turtle medicine from the depths of his compassionate soul. Adam is a Mestizo artisto—his work may be viewed at www.adamloya.wordpress.com.

Dawnee is a mystic living on the Gulf Islands of BC, Canada. She has practiced Healing Arts for 33 years to reclaim her Sacred Sexual Self. She is a passionate Tantric devotee and an aspiring Raw Food Chef. She offers the playful wisdom of the Dolphin Goddess.

Together, they create abundantly in spite of all obstacles. Transforming the darkness of their pain and suffering, they humbly offer you their Divine Love light.